MW01204070

Sally & George

IN THE BEGINNING

Knowing Who You Are In Christ

Dr. Keith & Laurie Nemec

Carpenter's Son Publishing

© 2012 Total Health Institute

Dr. Keith & Laurie Nemec

Front cover painted by Aaron Miller.

Cover and interior designed by Suzanne Lawing

All Bible quotes are from the King James Version.

All rights reserved. No part of this book may be reproduced or transmitted in any form or by any means, electronic or mechanical, including photocopying, recording or by any information storage and retrieval system, without permission in writing from the copyright owner.

Published by Carpenter's Son Publishing, Franklin, Tennessee

Published in association with Larry Carpenter of Christian Book Services, LLC

www.christianbookservices.com

978-0-9883043-0-7

This book is dedicated to our Family:
God our Father, Jesus Christ our Big Brother, Lord
and Savior, and the Holy Spirit our Teacher, Comforter
and the One who Empowers us on the journey of life.

The authors' writing style is that of a teacher, thus key concepts are purposely repeated throughout. If the mind is the gatekeeper to the heart, then the only way to break through is to keep speaking the Truth without ceasing. Through repetition, and with Perseverance, the Truth is driven past the gatekeeper, deep into the heart, to set the person free.

All references to God the Father, God the Son, Jesus Christ, or God the Holy Spirit, and the nature or attributes of God will be capitalized throughout this book (i.e., He, Truth, Peace, Grace, etc.).

All references to satan or sally & george will be purposely kept in lower case signifying their place of no authority.

All authors' comments in scripture text are enclosed in brackets [ ].

All bolded and underlined scripture text are to add authors' emphasis. They are not contained in the original text.

CHAPTERS

INTRODUCTION

The two things that have caused more debilitation, hardship, disability, suffering, and disease to all humanity since the beginning of time can be narrowed down to doubt and fear.

The purpose of this book is to expose the power of doubt; to expose the power of he who disguises himself as an angel of light and works his most destructive forces in the minds of those who listen to and believe his words.

Another purpose of this book is to show you the first step in freeing yourself from the fear and doubt in your life. In other words, to separate who you ARE from who you are NOT.

The foundation of everything is Truth. The reason doubt can enter your mind is because the Truth is questioned. Anything not of Truth is a lie. You can question facts, but Truth is beyond questioning.

God our Father created all things. He created the light and the darkness; He created the heavens and the earth. God's Name, His Nature, and His Word are all in agreement. God our Father created all life, including the Tree of Life and the tree of the knowledge of good and evil. He created these two trees with very specific purposes for each.

This book is about the part of each one of us that continually breaks the covenant relationship with God our Father in Heaven. It will show you how to overcome this part of yourself so you may once again live fully in the Love, Joy, Peace, and Hope that is rightfully yours when you are restored in the covenant of Love relationship with your Father in Heaven. This part of us is our old nature, our flesh, or our sin nature, and it lives apart from God. We call it sally & george.

1
WHO ARE SALLY & GEORGE?

sally & george are the random names we have given to the part of our minds, wills, desires, and emotions apart from God. You can use any name you like, as long as it is not your own name.

Your new nature is your God-like or Christ-like nature, which was made possible when Jesus Christ cut a new and everlasting covenant with His Father in Heaven. This covenant says that when a person becomes one with Christ by entering a covenant relationship with Him, their relationship and communion with God the Father in Heaven is restored.

If you have entered into the new and everlasting covenant with God your Father through His Son Jesus Christ, the Lord and Savior of all humanity, you live with two natures. One nature is of God and is filled with His Holy Spirit and led by the Truth-filled heart. The other nature is apart from God and led by the ego-driven (I, me, my, mine) mind. This ego-driven nature is sally & george.

Who you are is a new nature in Christ that also contains and old nature apart from Christ. Both natures co-exist, but one rules in every moment of your life. When you are ruled by your sally or george—your old mind, old will, old desires, and old emotions—then your new nature, Christ within your heart, is like the light of the Sun covered by a basket. When you are ruled by your Truth-filled heart—your new nature in Christ, filled with the Holy Spirit, the Spirit of your Father in Heaven—then you are a reflection, an exact representation of your Father in Heaven and although you still have an old nature, it does not rule or control you in that moment.

Scenarios

Another way to see who sally & george are is to consider how they operate in situations such as the following:

1. A husband and wife who both love the Lord with all their heart get a divorce after twenty years of marriage. How can this be?

2. A man asks Jesus into his heart and receives His salvation. He experiences the Joy of the Lord and is filled with His Holy Spirit. Life is beautiful beyond description. The man is truly a new creation. Yet, two years later this man is fearful, doubtful, and depressed, and he now questions if he knows Jesus and is saved. How can this be?

3. A man who has loved the Lord for the last thirty years suddenly loses his business. He remains jobless, with no income, for five years and loses all that he has, ending up homeless. He becomes bitter and angry with God for what has happened to him. How can this be?

4. A woman of faith knows the power of prayer, and she prays day and night for her sick father to heal from cancer. Despite her prayers, her father's condition does not change. He soon dies. This woman starts to question her faith and wonders if God is really there in her time of need. She even questions if God really exists. How can this be?

5. A man knows and loves Jesus. He has spent his life serving the Lord faithfully when, all of a sudden, he is diagnosed with a brain tumor and given six months to live. He has chemotherapy and radiation but only worsens. As his energy and mind start to fade, he cries out to God for the reason this disease has not healed. Growing closer to the end, his thoughts are filled with doubt, fear, and confusion. His unanswered questions cause him to sink into depression, and he loses all hope. How can this be?

In each of these scenarios, the old nature—sally or george—gained a foothold when a person chose to believe a lie instead of the Truth. Once sally & george have overpowered a person's Truth-filled heart, they begin to rule behavior from the ego-filled mind. The heart of Truth, of Love, of Joy, and of Peace becomes covered, hardened, and taken captive by a self-centered (I, me, my, mine) world- and fact-filled mind. This book will empower you to live life to the full in body, mind, and spirit, and show you how to break free from the fear and doubt of your old nature. You will learn to fully live the command of our Lord Jesus Christ when He said:

John 14:12-13

> *Verily, verily, I say unto you, He that believeth on me* [entering the new and everlasting covenant through Jesus, the covenant representative], *the works that I do shall he do also; and greater works than these shall he do* [you will do everything Jesus did, and more, because He will be in you and His Holy Spirit will do these works through you]; *because I go unto my Father.*

> *And whatsoever ye shall ask in my name, that will I do, that the Father may be glorified in the Son* [you may ask anything in the name of Jesus, as long as it brings glory to the Father; meaning it is doing His will, not your sally or george ego-filled will].

John 8:31-32

> *Then said Jesus to those Jews which believed on him, If ye continue in my word* [if you are in covenant with God the Father through the covenant representative Jesus Christ, and if you continue in His Word by following your Truth-filled heart rather than your sally or george mind], *then are ye my disciples indeed;*

> *And ye shall know the truth* [who is Jesus Christ, and the revelation knowledge that comes through the Holy Spirit],

and the truth [Jesus Christ] *shall make you free.*

Why must you call your old nature a name other than your own?

You must have a clear-cut separation between who you are in your God nature, being "in Christ," and who you appear to be because of your old nature. This separation must not only be called by a different name, but spoken of by that name. This brings the Truth into the physical realm.

Rom 10:9-10

> *That if thou shalt confess with thy mouth the Lord Jesus, and shalt believe in thine heart that God hath raised him from the dead, thou shalt be saved.*
>
> *For with the heart man believeth unto righteousness; and with the mouth confession is made unto salvation.*

To clarify this concept, let us use eating a cookie as an example:

When you desire a cookie ask yourself, "Who wants to eat this cookie loaded with sugar and refined flour?"

Does your body want the cookie? Yes or no? If you said yes, let us get much more specific:

1. Does your liver want the cookie?
2. Does your pancreas want the cookie?
3. Does your small intestine want the cookie?

Now let us go from organs and glands to systems:

1. Does your nervous system want the cookie?
2. Does your immune system want the cookie?
3. Does your hormonal system want the cookie?
4. Does your digestive system want the cookie?
5. Does your elimination system want the cookie?

Now we will ask again: does your body want the cookie? The answer is obvious: absolutely not.

Who we are (a new creation in Christ) as compared to who we appear to be (old creation apart from Christ- sally and george)

The square represents our old nature apart from God/Christ- This is sally and george, the old unrenewed mind.

The star represents our new nature being one with God/Christ- This is who we were created by God to be. The Spirit-filled and directed heart.

Who you are is a new nature in Christ that also contains an old nature apart from Christ- sally or george. Both natures co-exist but one always rules in each moment of your life.

When you are ruled by your sally or george old mind, old will, old desires, and old emotions, then your new nature, which is Christ within your heart is like a brilliant light covered by a basket.

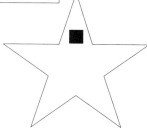

When you are ruled by your Christ-filled heart, your new nature in Christ, filled with the Holy Spirit, then you are the reflection of your Father in Heaven and although you still have an old nature, it does not control you anymore.

The next question: does your spirit want the cookie?

Does the part of you who was made to communicate and commune with God, and whose job it is to hear from God and oversee the total health of the body and mind, want the cookie?

The answer is found in the purpose of the spirit of man. God breathed the breath of life into man, and it became man's spirit. If the spirit or heart (as it is also called) is the communion/communication channel from God to you, then why would God put it in your heart to eat cookies? Does eating cookies glorify God, or does eating cookies indulge the self, the "I, me, my, mine" nature apart from Christ?

Understanding that the heart is equivalent to the spirit is important; they are one and the same.

Ezek 36:26

> A **new heart** also will I give you, and a **new spirit** will I put within you: and I will take away the stony heart [the hard heart means the sally & george mind is blocking the Truth from being spoken into your heart] out of your flesh, and I will give you an heart of flesh [a heart that is alive and filled with the Holy Spirit of Truth].

This verse tells us a new heart is the same as a new spirit, or that your heart is the same as your spirit.

Ps 51:17

> The sacrifices of God are a **broken spirit: a broken and a contrite heart...**

We are told that a broken spirit is the same as a broken heart.

John 7:37-39

> In the last day, that great day of the feast, Jesus stood and cried, saying, If any man thirst, let him come unto me, and drink.

*He that believeth on me, as the scripture hath said, out of his **belly** [the word belly is also translated as heart] shall flow rivers of living water.*

*(**But this spake he of the** [Holy] **Spirit,** which they that believe on him should receive: for the Holy [Spirit] Ghost was not yet given; because that Jesus was not yet glorified.)*

The Holy Spirit flows from your heart, from your spirit.

You may ask, then, if your spirit/heart does not want the cookie, and your body does not want the cookie, then who does?

sally & george do!

To summarize, your body is the temple of God's Holy Spirit and, as such, wants only food to make the body healthy so you may fulfill your purpose in this life. Your spirit/heart is your communication channel with God where He speaks to you so you may do His will instead of your old nature's will. Instead of your flesh-filled, ego-filled, world-filled, five senses-filled—sally- & george-filled will.

Why does your mind want the cookie? Well, it does and it doesn't. Let's look at the division of who you ARE, and who you are NOT.

Who you are IN CHRIST in your new nature; your mind of Christ, your will of Christ, your desire of Christ, and your emotions of Christ.	Who you are apart from CHRIST in your old nature; old mind, old will, old desires, and old emotions.
Perfect mind of Christ.	Imperfect mind of the old nature.
Do the will of your Father in Heaven.	Do your own will.
Desire of the heart is to do His will.	Desire of the mind is to do your will.
Emotion or energy in motion of compassion and passion for what He puts into your heart.	Emotion or energy in motion of pleasure, gratification, and happiness that drives your mind.

Your old mind, old will, old desire, and old emotion want the cookie because pleasure is what feeds them.

2 Tim 3:1-5

> *This know also, that in the last days perilous times shall come. For men* [and women who are living from their sally & george old natures] *shall be lovers of their own selves, covetous, boasters, proud, blasphemers, disobedient to parents, unthankful, unholy,*

> *Without natural affection, trucebreakers, false accusers, incontinent, fierce, despisers of those that are good,*

> *Traitors, heady, highminded, **lovers of pleasures more than lovers of God;***

> *Having a form of godliness, but denying the power thereof: from such turn away.*

Phil 3:18-19

> *(For many walk, of whom I have told you often, and now tell you even weeping, that they* [those who are living from their sally or george old nature] *are the enemies of the cross of Christ:*

> *Whose end is destruction, **whose God is their belly,** and whose glory is in their shame, **who mind earthly things*** [they are letting sally & george thoughts totally control them, by thinking only about themselves and things of the world].)

Why is separation from the old nature so important?

You are called to be separate from everything which does not honor God your Father in Heaven and glorify Jesus Christ, His Son and your most precious covenant representative to the Father. But let us go deeper with this concept. You are also called to be separate from the old nature within who does not honor your Father in Heaven and glorify

Jesus Christ, and who does not put Jesus on the throne of your life (who does not live from their Christ-like new nature as One with the Father in Heaven, but instead lives from their sally or george old nature, the "I, me, my, mine" old nature).

2 Cor 6:16-7:1

> *And what agreement hath the temple of God with idols? for ye are the temple of the living God* [your body is the temple of the Holy Spirit. It is to be used to praise, worship, honor, and glorify God]; *as God hath said, I will dwell in them, and walk in them; and I will be their God, and they shall be my people.*

> *Wherefore come out from among them, and be ye separate, saith the Lord, and touch not the unclean thing; and I will receive you.*

> *And will be a Father unto you, and ye shall be my sons and daughters, saith the Lord Almighty.*

> *Having therefore these promises, dearly beloved, let us cleanse ourselves from all filthiness of the flesh and spirit* [this is the sally or george old nature], *perfecting holiness* [being fully "in Christ" each moment] *in the fear of God* [giving God all reverence, honor, and glory].

What contaminates the body and spirit? The old nature, old mind, old will, old desires, and old emotions, and those people filled with and led by the old nature. This is sally & george!

In our journey, we realized another nature was living in us who had a different agenda for life than we do.

So what is our agenda, purpose, and plan in this life? Let us start at the beginning.

In the Garden of Eden were two trees, the Tree of Life and the tree of the knowledge of good and evil. These two trees represent the whole human journey and experience.

• **The Tree of Life**—represents your covenant relationship with God your Father in Heaven, and also living a heart-directed life in and from Him. This is the We—the Christ and me who have become One—like a covenant marriage relationship where the two have become one, or a blood brother relationship where the two have become one.

- **The tree of the knowledge of good and evil (bad)**—represents our covenant with satan after breaking our original covenant with God in the Garden. This is a self-directed life trying to put the "I, me, my, mine" old nature, mind, will, desires, and emotions on the throne of your life. It is trying to be God as satan tries to be God.

The tree of the knowledge of good and evil's ultimate purpose is to show us we cannot live this life apart from God. This leads us back to God the Father through the Savior, who is Jesus Christ.

So who are sally & george? They are our old nature apart from God. They represent living for and from ourselves instead of for and from God.

To better understand the two trees in the Garden, you need a more complete understanding of what each represents.

The Tree of Life represents eternal life—the God-filled and God-directed life where you are One with Him. It represents having the Spirit of God within your heart and being led, empowered, and directed by the Holy Spirit. This is the source of true Love, Joy, Peace, and Hope.

Jer 31:33

> *But this shall be the covenant that I will make. . .saith the* LORD, *I will put my law* [of the Spirit of Life, not the law of sin and death] *in their inward parts* [also translated as heart or belly], *and write it in their hearts; and will be their God, and they shall be my people.*

On the other hand, the tree of the knowledge of good and evil represents the life apart from a covenant relationship with God the Father through His Son, Jesus Christ, the new and everlasting covenant representative. This is the life lived from your mind, your will, your ability, your talent, your desire, your emotions, and with your timing.

This is the life where you are in control (so you think) and you seek comfort, pleasure, power, and to be happy. The problem with this tree is it always has two sides. Good and bad, happy and sad. You cannot have one without the other. So with this tree, you are constantly trying to make your life a certain way, yet even when you feel as if you have temporarily made it because now you are really happy and life is going really well, all of a sudden your happiness-in-a-flash becomes sad, and your good becomes bad.

In life, you have three choices, but actually just two. You can choose God, good, or bad. However, we have noted that good and bad are actually one choice together. You may choose the Tree of Life in this moment, or you may choose the tree of the knowledge of good and evil (bad). Simply stated, you have three doors to choose from: door number 1 is God, door number 2 is the good side of the tree of knowledge of good and evil (bad), and door number 3 is the bad, or evil, side of the tree of knowledge of good and evil. So think which door—number 1, 2, or 3— you are going to choose with everything that comes into your life?

Here is an example: A person fasts and prays, expecting God to hear his prayer. Which door is he in? It is door number 2 because he is doing something good to get something in return. This is living in cause and effect, sowing and reaping.

Another example: A person has very low self-esteem, feeling like they will never accomplish anything in life because they lack any talent or ability. Which door is it? Door number 3.

How about this example: A person feels an overwhelming Peace in making a decision that should not be peaceful. Their thoughts tell of all they will lose if they go forward with this decision, yet they still have a Peace they cannot explain. Which door is this? That is right, door number 1. So remember to always be aware of what door you are in or what tree you are in.

Door Number 1	Door Number 2	Door Number 3
Tree of Life	Tree of knowledge of good	Tree of knowledge of evil (bad)

God	good	bad
Eternal Life	life	death
Joy unspeakable	happy	sad
Peace that transcends all understanding	peaceful	stressful
Unconditional Love	conditional love	hate
Hope in Him, the anchor of our soul, the Rock	hopeful	hopeless
Truth	fact	lie
Know that you know that you know	knowledge	doubt
Trust	courage	fear
Covenant relationship with God through Christ	religion	evil

The most accurate description of the old nature (sally & george) apart from the new nature "in Christ" is given by the apostle Paul in a letter to the church in Rome:

Rom 7:15-25

> *For that which I do I allow not: for what I would, that do I not; but what I hate, that do I.*
>
> *If then I do that which I would not, I consent unto the law that it is good.*
>
> **Now then it is no more I that do it, but sin that dwelleth in me** [I am not doing it but george is doing it in me].
>
> *For I know that in me (that is, in my flesh* [in my old george nature, apart from Christ]*,) dwelleth no good thing: for to will is present with me; but how to perform that which is good I find not.*
>
> *For the good that I would I do not: but the evil which I*

would not, that I do.

Now if I do that I would not, it is no more I that do it, but sin that dwelleth in me [I am not doing the action. The old nature, george, apart from Christ, is controlling me in that moment and doing the action or saying the words].

I find then a law, that, when I would do good, evil is present with me.

For I delight in the law of God [the Law of the Spirit of Life] *after the inward man:*

But I see another law [the law of sin and death] *in my members, warring against the law of my mind* [mind of Christ and heart of Christ within me], *and bringing me into captivity to the law of sin which is in my members.*

O wretched man that I am! [When I am living from my old george nature apart from Christ, instead of living from my new nature "in Christ"] *who shall deliver me from the body of this death* [from the control that george has over me]?

I thank God through Jesus Christ our Lord. So then with the mind [of Christ within me] *I myself serve the law of God* [the Law of the Spirit of Life]; *but with the flesh* [the old george nature] *the law of sin* [and death].

The law has but one purpose in the New Testament: to lead us to Christ.

As stated in Gal 3:19-25

Wherefore then serveth the law [what was the purpose of the law]? *It was added because of transgressions, till the seed* [Jesus Christ] *should come to whom the promise was made;. . .*

Is the law then against the promises of God? God forbid: **for if there had been a law given which could have given** *life, verily righteousness should have been by the law.*

But the scripture hath concluded all under sin [the sally & george old nature]*, that the promise by faith of Jesus Christ might be given to them that believe.*

But before faith came, we were kept under the law, shut up unto the faith which should afterwards be revealed.

Wherefore the law was our schoolmaster to bring us unto Christ, that we might be justified by faith [trusting in Jesus Christ as the new and everlasting covenant representative].

But after that faith is come, we are no longer under a schoolmaster [we have been set free from the law of sin and death and are now only living from the Law of the Spirit of Life in Christ].

So, once again, who are sally & george?

According to Paul, the sinful nature, or flesh nature, apart from Christ lives in us. Our sin nature is not our true self, but is our old nature apart from the nature of God which we have when we truly are in Christ. Understand Paul's important words when he says he is not sinning—he is not the old nature, but instead the old nature (george) is doing the sinning while inhabiting his body. The old nature (george) is the voice in his head tempting him to live in the part of him that is separate from God. The old nature (george) is a wretched man.

Is Paul a wretched man? No.

The old nature does not have to leave for you to live in Victory and Freedom. When you live from your Truth-filled heart in Christ, separating from your old nature, you will have Victory over sally & george. Even more powerful is the Truth that nothing can ever separate you from the Love of God, even when sally & george overpower you, causing you to fall in the moment. Knowing these truths enables you to live a life of Victory and Freedom in Christ:

1. In your weakness is where His strength, His Holy Spirit, manifests.

2. No condemnation exists for those who are in Christ Jesus.

3. Nothing can ever separate you from the Love of God.

Now, some would say "what about 2 Corinthians 5:17 when it says the old nature has gone?"

2 Cor 5:17

Therefore if any man be in Christ [in the new and everlasting covenant, having Jesus as his/her covenant representative], *he is a new creature* [he/she now has a mind and heart of Christ, filled with the Holy Spirit]*: old things are passed away* [sally & george no longer have control to sit on the throne of your life]; *behold, all things are become new.*

The meaning of this scripture has to flow synergistically with Paul's explanation of his wretched old nature living within him apart from Christ. What has gone is not the old nature, but the authority the old nature has once you have come to Christ and become a new nature "in Christ." In your new nature, you have free will and may choose to live from your Christ-like nature each moment instead of being kept in bondage to the old nature and letting it rule your life.

When you are in your new nature in Christ, you are perfect. This perfection is not based on your good works, nor on anything you can do, but on Jesus Christ's perfection and what He did at the cross.

Matt 5:48

Be ye therefore perfect, even as your Father which is in heaven is perfect.

This is why you must take your eyes off sally & george and put them on Jesus; your Rock, your Foundation, your Perfection. With man and woman it is impossible, but with God all things are Possible. Who you actually are is not who you think you are. Who you are is who He IS. That is why you are called a Christian.

Also know when you are commanded to "Be perfect, even as your Father which is in heaven is perfect" it is not a call to do more, pray more, work harder, go to church more, or read more of your Bible (these would be door 2—good and religious sally & george). No, this is a call to be who you are in Christ—perfect—instead of who you are in your old sally or george nature, apart from Christ—imperfect.

Most people live 95% of their day in their old sally or george nature, and only 5% in their new nature, being "in Christ."

Not Just Once

This decision to be "in Christ" has to be made every moment of your life after you receive Him as your Lord and Savior (Lord meaning He is your covenant representative to the Father in Heaven, He is your everything; and Savior meaning only His cutting the new and everlasting covenant allows you to be set free from your sally or george nature).

To be "clothed with Christ" is not a one-time decision. Instead, you are to put Him on or wear Him each moment of your life by following the Truth your Father in Heaven speaks to your heart through the Holy Spirit. Each moment you can choose eternal life "in Christ," or you can choose death by following the old sally or george mind.

When you decide to follow Christ will all of your old nature be permanently gone?

No. First, God made us in His own image and likeness, and in being like Him we have free will in deciding each moment of our lives. The most important choice is this: am I going to follow the Truth I know God is speaking into my heart, or am I going to follow the lies, facts, and knowledge sally or george and the world system apart from God are speaking into my sally or george mind?

Second, sally & george play a very important role in your life. They do have a purpose, and they will continue to fulfill their purpose until you are no longer physically present on the planet.

When you choose to be "in Christ" each moment, choosing NOT to be in the flesh or the old nature of sally or george that moment, you are choosing eternal life instead. In doing so, you are constantly crucifying, or putting to death, the sally or george old nature moment by moment.

To crucify sally or george you must always be fully alert, fully awake, fully aware, and on guard because the enemy wants to devour and destroy you, and he can do this if his agents sally & george are allowed to control your mind, your will, your desires, and your emotions.

Didn't we crucify the old nature when we came to Christ?

Gal 2:20-21

> *I am crucified with Christ* [my old sally or george nature has been nailed to the cross]: *nevertheless I live; yet not I* [good and bad, sally & george, have no more authority over me when I choose to be in my new Christ nature], *but Christ liveth in me: and the life which I now live in the flesh* [this body] *I live by the faith* [trust] *of the Son of God, who loved me, and gave himself for me.*

> *I do not frustrate the grace of God: for if righteousness come by the law* [by doing good works in good sally or george—door number 2], *then Christ is dead in vain* [Jesus' sacrificial death to establish the new and everlasting covenant of Grace was all for nothing].

What are the actions of the old nature?

Gal 5:19-21

> *Now the works of the flesh* [sally or george nature] *are manifest, which are these; Adultery, fornication, uncleanness, lasciviousness* [lustfulness],

> *Idolatry* [anything in your life you worship or give greater value than God], *witchcraft,* [quarrels, jealousy, outbursts of passion, rivalries, dissensions] *hatred, variance, emulations, wrath, strife, seditions* [divisions], *heresies,*

> *Envyings, murders, drunkenness, revellings, and such like: of the which I tell you before, as I have also told you in time past, that they which do such things shall not inherit the kingdom of God.*

So, the answer to the question of "Didn't we crucify the old nature when we came to Christ?" is yes *and* no. In Christ, the old nature has been nailed to the cross, but your old nature is a deceiver and will speak lies to you. He or she will try to tempt you to eat from the tree of the knowledge of good and evil once again—especially door number 2. Your sally or george will try to come off that cross by using words such as these:

"Did God really say that?"

"Are you really done with sin?"

"Are you really a Christian?"

The answer is found in what salvation means:

I was saved—by the blood of Jesus Christ. All my sin nature, my sally or george nature, has been put to death on the cross. She/he has been nailed to the cross.

I am being saved—meaning I am in the process of fighting the good fight against the old sally or george nature because she/he keeps trying to come off the cross and come back to life, even though Jesus has put them to death. I must continually nail sally or george back on the cross moment by moment.

I will be saved—meaning at the appointed time my earthly physical existence will end permanently and so will sally & george, never again to exist in my eternity.

The resurrected life can only come with a crucified life. We cannot experience the power of resurrection unless we continually crucify our old nature.

What does the crucified life mean?

Jesus said we must die to ourselves, to our old sally or george natures, in order to live an eternal life in the here and now. We must keep nailing our old sally or george nature to the cross daily even moment by moment.

Luke 9:23-24

> *And he said to them all, If any man will come after me, let him deny himself* [sally's or george's desire to do their own will instead of God's will]*, and take up his cross **daily**,*

[nail sally or george to the cross moment by moment] *and follow me.*

For whosoever will save his life [trying to live from good sally or george thoughts, words, and actions] *shall lose it: but whosoever will lose his life for my sake* [crucifies sally & george every moment], *the same shall save it* [will be living in Christ, not in the old nature].

John 12:24-26

Verily [This is the Truth], *verily* [This is the Truth], *I say unto you, Except a corn of wheat fall into the ground and die, it abideth alone: but if it die, it bringeth forth much fruit.*

He that loveth his life [good sally or george] *shall lose it; and he that hateth his life in this world* [hates sally or george trying to control and sit on the throne of her/his life] *shall keep it unto life eternal.*

If any man serve me, let him follow me; and where I am, there shall also my servant be: if any man serve me, him will my Father honour.

Rom 6:5-23

For if we have been planted together in the likeness of his death, we shall be also in the likeness of his resurrection:

Knowing this, that our old man [sally's or george's power over us] *is crucified with him, that the body of sin might be destroyed, that henceforth we should not serve sin* [sally or george in this moment].

For he that is dead is freed from sin [in Christ you are dead to sally's or george's power over you].

Now if we be dead with Christ, we believe that we shall also live with him [live fully in our new Christ nature, being empowered by the Holy Spirit]:

Knowing that Christ being raised from the dead dieth no more; death hath no more dominion over him.

For in that he died, he died unto sin once: but in that he liveth, he liveth unto God.

Likewise reckon ye also yourselves to be dead indeed unto sin [dead to the power that sally & george have over you], *but alive unto God through Jesus Christ our Lord* [this is eternal life in your new nature].

Let not sin therefore reign in your mortal body [do not choose to let sally or george take control of each moment], *that ye should obey it in the lusts thereof.*

Neither yield ye your members as instruments of unrighteousness unto sin [do not let sally or george rule your mind and body]*: but yield yourselves unto God, as those that are alive from the dead, and your members as instruments of righteousness unto God* [let your Christ nature rule each moment].

For sin [sally & george thoughts, words, and actions] *shall not have dominion over you: for ye are not under the law* [the control of sally & george speaking to your mind, the law of sin and death, doors numbered 2 and 3]*, but under grace* [the control of Christ speaking to your heart, the Law of the Spirit of Life, door number 1].

What then? shall we sin [live from sally & george]*, because we are not under the law, but under grace? God forbid.*

Know ye not, that to whom ye yield yourselves servants to obey, his servants ye are to whom ye obey; whether of sin [slaves of sally & george thoughts, words, and actions] *unto death, or of obedience* [willfully choosing to follow your new nature in Christ, your Truth- and Spirit-filled heart] *unto righteousness?*

But God be thanked, that ye were the servants of sin [under the control of sally & george], *but ye have obeyed from the heart that form of doctrine which was delivered you* [you accepted Jesus into your heart and were saved in body, mind, and spirit].

Being then made free from sin [the control sally or george once had over your life], *ye became the servants of righteousness* [under control of your Spirit-filled heart in your new nature in Christ].

I speak after the manner of men because of the infirmity of your flesh [sally & george so want to control your life]*: for as ye have yielded your members servants to uncleanness and to iniquity unto iniquity; even so now yield your members servants to righteousness unto holiness.*

For when ye were the servants of sin [you had no choice but to do what sally or george told you to do], *ye were free from righteousness* [you did not yet have a new nature, so you could not follow a Truth-filled heart].

What fruit had ye then in those things whereof ye are now ashamed? for the end of those things is death.

But now being made free from sin [the power sally or george had over your life], *and become servants to God* [being led by your new heart, your new nature in Christ, and being empowered by His Holy Spirit], *ye have your fruit unto holiness* [all the fruit of the Holy Spirit in your life in the here and now], *and the end everlasting life* [eternal life in Heaven].

For the wages of sin [letting sally or george control this moment in your life] *is death* [separation from the Truth]*; but the gift of God is eternal life* [when you are fully in Christ in each moment] *through Jesus Christ our Lord.*

sally & george are agents of the devil, and they have one agenda in your life: to sit upon the throne of your life.

John 10:10

The thief cometh not, but for to steal, and to kill, and to destroy: I am come that they might have life, and that they might have it more abundantly [this is eternal life, being in a covenant relationship with God, and being a member of the Family of God].

The thief is satan, and satan's connection within you, sally or george. What are sally & george going to steal, kill, and destroy?

sally & george have come to steal the Truth by luring you into following their lies, and the facts of the mind and the world system.

They have come to kill all the manifestations of the Holy Spirit-filled life: to kill His Love, His Joy, His Peace, His Hope, His Power in you, by counterfeiting them. They accomplish this by making you think they are like the world system's conditional love, the system's false happiness, its false peacefulness and false hope. Most detrimentally, they have come to destroy your relationship with your Father in Heaven by keeping you distracted, focused on yourself, your sally or george nature. Sitting on the throne of your life, they prevent you from keeping your eyes fixed on your first Love, your Father in Heaven, your covenant representative Jesus Christ, and God who lives within you—the Holy Spirit. They may even speak doubt into your mind when life does not go as you expected, saying things such as: "Is God really interested in me?" "Is God always going to be there to help me when I am in need?" They may even go to the extreme of blaming God for the negative things happening in your life.

The greatest desire of the old nature is to separate you from God, ensuring their power and authority over you. When you have separated from God (though He never separates from you), you have become one with sally or george, and their lies will rule your life. Just like the cookie.

Can we separate from God in our mind? Yes. Can He separate from us? Do our actions change His Love for us? Absolutely not! God's

Love for us is unconditional and never-ending. We know this because He sent His Son to die for us when we were sinners, living completely in our sally and george natures, when we were separate from Him.

Rom 8:35-39

> *Who shall separate us from the love of Christ? shall tribu-lation, or distress, or persecution, or famine, or nakedness, or peril, or sword?*

> *As it is written, For thy sake we are killed all the day long; we are accounted as sheep for the slaughter.*

> *Nay, in all these things we are more than conquerors through him that loved us.*

> *For I am persuaded, that neither death, nor life, nor an-gels, nor principalities, nor powers, nor things present, nor things to come,*

> *Nor height, nor depth, nor any other creature* [including sally & george], *shall be able to separate us from the love of God, which is in Christ Jesus our Lord.*

1 Peter 5:8-9

> *Be sober* [walking in the fruit of the Holy Spirit, which is self-control], *be vigilant* [be awake, alert, and aware]; *because your adversary the devil* [and his offspring—the sally & george mind], *as a roaring lion, walketh about, seeking whom he may devour:*

> *Whom resist* [the devil and sally & george] *stedfast in the faith* [stand firm against him, strong in your trust in God the Father, God the Son, and God the Holy Spirit];. . .

You cannot take your eyes off God your Father, even for one mo-ment, because if you do, your enemy, the sally or george old nature, will devour you, and you will live the sally & george filled life from the old mind, will, desire, and emotions instead of the Holy Spirit filled life from your heart of Truth being "in Christ." Never forget the word faith means "trust," so what you are standing firm in is your trust in what Jesus did for you by becoming the covenant representative with the Father in Heaven, so all who come to Him can live "in Christ" and in the Truth and Power of His Holy Spirit each moment of their life.

Rom 8:5-9

For they that are after the flesh [sally & george mind, will, emotions, words, and actions] *do mind the things of the flesh* [sally & george nature apart from Christ]*; but they that are after the Spirit* [being in Christ, in the new covenant, and being filled with the Holy Spirit] *the things of the Spirit.*

For to be carnally minded [men and woman who are ruled by sally & george] *is death* [separation from the Truth]*; but to be spiritually minded* [the mind of Christ within you] *is life and peace.*

Because the carnal [sally & george] *mind is enmity against God* [sally & george are against God being on the throne of your life, because they desire to be on the throne]*: for it is not subject to the law of God, neither indeed can be.*

So then they that are in the flesh [sally & george filled mind, will, desires, emotions, words, and actions] *cannot please God.*

But ye are not in the flesh [no longer under the power of sally & george]*, but in the* [Holy] *Spirit, if so be that the Spirit of God dwell in you* [if you have entered the covenant relationship with your Father in Heaven through His covenant representative, who is Jesus Christ].

Gal 5:16-18

This I say then, Walk in the Spirit [being in Christ and empowered by the Holy Spirit], *and ye shall not fulfil the lust of the flesh* [sally & george].

For the flesh lusteth against the Spirit, and the Spirit against the flesh [sally & george and the Holy Spirit are at war for control over you]*: and these are contrary the one to the other: so that ye cannot do the things that ye would* [if you allow sally & george to win the war in any moment, you are blocking the power of the Holy Spirit].

But if ye be led of the Spirit [submitting to the Holy Spirit so that He is winning the war in the moment and His Power is magnified. This is when you are in the Tree of Life, being fully "in Christ"], *ye are not under the law* [of sin and death, not living from the tree of the knowledge of good and evil anymore].

Gal 5:22-26

But the fruit of the [Holy] *Spirit* [living from your heart of Truth; being in Christ] *is Love, Joy, Peace, Longsuffering* [Patience], *Gentleness, Goodness, Faith, Meekness, Temperance* [Self-Control]*: against such there is no law* [you are not in bondage to the tree of the knowledge of good and evil—the law of sin and death—when you submit to the control of the Holy Spirit].

And they that are Christ's have crucified the flesh [and continue to crucify and nail sally & george to the cross, putting them to death moment by moment] *with the affections and lusts* [and all their control over us, when we choose Christ each moment].

If we live in the [Holy] *Spirit* [being led by our Truth-filled heart rather than our fact- and lie-filled mind], *let us also walk in the Spirit* [every moment letting the Holy Spirit do and say God's will through our body and our tongue with His action, His Word, on His timing].

Let us not be desirous of vain glory, provoking one another, envying one another [let us not give control of our life back to sally or george].

The attributes of God your Father come to you through the Power of His Holy Spirit living within your heart and renewing your mind to be the mind of Christ within you. These are the fruit of the Holy Spirit. When you are "in Christ" (in the new and everlasting blood covenant love relationship with your Father in Heaven), and you are obeying and guarding the Truth the Holy Spirit speaks to your heart, you are eating from the Tree of Life instead of the tree of the knowledge of good and evil. When you eat from the Tree of Life, you receive the Blessing and Power of the Spirit of God manifesting in your life (this is door number 1). When you eat from the tree of the knowledge of good and evil, you find constant suffering from living apart from God, instead living in the good/bad and happy/sad cycle of that old tree. This is living constantly from doors 2 and 3. To fully understand who you ARE "in Christ" as opposed to who you are NOT in your old sally or george nature you must understand what a covenant is and who you are in the new covenant.

2
WHAT IS A COVENANT RELATIONSHIP?

What is a covenant?

In ancient times (and even today in some parts of the world) tribes of people entered into the most binding relationship possible. They entered into a covenant relationship. Some of the main points of the covenant relationship included the following.

Two parties entered an agreement to strengthen their weakness, and the agreement lasted at least eight generations. Therefore, this agreement was not taken lightly, because the party or tribe of people you bonded with would be tied for at least eight generations to your family. The bond was taken for life and death, and was always accompanied by the shedding of blood and taking of oaths or promises.

The covenant must be maintained even if it cost you your life. In these covenants, any one person would gladly give his or her life upholding the covenant if someone harmed their covenant partner. A covenant was permanent and could not be broken. On the extremely rare occasion when a covenant was broken, one party HAD TO kill the other party as payment for the breaking of the covenant. They had no choice in this; it must be done or the covenant would have no power. The foundation of the covenant was love and the building up of each other, with no way out of the covenant but death.

What is a covenant made of?

- **Promises**—these are the terms of the covenant, meaning this is what I am swearing on my very life, and the lives of at least eight generations of my offspring, I will do for you.
- **Shedding of blood**—a sacrificial animal is killed as a part of the covenant agreement.
- **Seal**—this is the permanent sign of the covenant relationship for all to see.

Thus, if two tribes decided to covenant together, they essentially became one tribe, receiving each other's strengths, and eliminating their weaknesses (promise of blessings). For instance, if one tribe was very wise, but not strong enough to defend themselves, that tribe would enter a covenant with a tribe that was very strong but perhaps not so wise. In this way, the two tribes would become essentially one tribe, combining the strengths of each, and in doing so minimizing their weaknesses.

Once the two tribes decided to enter a covenant, the terms were agreed upon. Each tribe's strengths were stated, and a reminder would be given that there was no breaking of the covenant; if one tribe broke the covenant the other tribe must fulfill the covenant agreement by killing the other tribe (shedding of blood, promise of cursing). Bloodshed was promised not out of hate, but out of respect for the power of the covenant agreement.

In the "cutting of the covenant," as it was called, it was acknowledged that those who are in covenant have a closer bond than natural brothers. This is the origin of the term blood brothers, as well as the saying that blood is thicker than water and milk. Your blood covenant brother is more your brother than the brother from your mother's womb and breast (water meaning amniotic fluid and milk representing breast milk). This is because you have entered into this covenant agreement through your own free will, whereas you had no choice of your birth brothers.

For this cutting of the covenant, each tribe would choose a representative, a person who embodied that tribe. For instance, if the tribe were great warriors, he would be the greatest of all the warriors. In essence, that person was "the tribe" and as a tribe (nation) they are all "in him."

Following choosing of the covenant representatives, weapons and gifts would be exchanged to symbolize a pledging of strengths, loyalty, and one's life to the covenant brother.

Next a young bull was sacrificed and split in half down the middle. The two covenant representatives would walk between the bloody halves in a figure eight pattern. This had the symbolic meaning of: "I will become your protection, I will assume your responsibility, I will take your place, I will in essence become 'you,' I will keep this covenant even if it kills me, and if I break this covenant, may I be killed and cut to pieces as this animal has been." This sacrifice of a young bull was not a sadistic or insensitive act, but rather a symbol of their commitment. In ancient days, the animals a tribe owned were their life blood. The animals were guarded carefully because they meant everything to the tribe. If their animals died, the tribe would eventually die. So the sacrifice of the best young bull represented giving of the very best they had to this covenant agreement. To these tribes, it was the same as giving their lives to uphold the covenant relationship.

Following the ritual slaughter, each tribe representative, still standing between the halves of the sacrificed bull, would recite an oath to uphold the terms of the covenant. Once thus stated, the terms could never be revoked. It was irrevocable and could never be cancelled.

The terms of the covenant were then put into writing, signed, and sealed before witnesses, then read publicly.

After the public reading of the terms, an incision was made on each covenant representative's right forearm or palm. Their two forearms or palms were then joined together, causing their blood to flow together as one. Blood always represented life. The two lives became one, and the two tribes became one. These scars were visible reminders of the covenant. Many times the covenant representative would put irritating substances in the wound to make the scar more pronounced once it healed.

The visible scar also served as a warning for anyone intending to harm any member of the covenant. Seeing the covenant scar, they would know that any harm done to this person is also being done to this person's covenant partner or tribe. An enemy would know they would pay the price of any injury to this person, as the covenant partner or tribe would seek retribution for any injury. Such a visible warning prevented many harmful acts because, in essence, harming any one member of a covenant relationship meant living with the uncertainty of how much harm the covenant partners would do to you and your tribe in return. Covenant relationships kept the peace.

After the covenant wound was made, the next act was the exchange of names. For example, the Smith tribe would now be called the Smith-Jones tribe, and the Jones tribe would permanently become the Jones-Smith tribe. The two tribes had become one tribe.

One of the final acts of the covenant relationship agreement was the covenant meal, the eating of bread and drinking of wine. Symbolically, this breaking of bread meant, "as you eat this bread, my body and all contained in it is yours, or my body will be given, even broken if necessary, for you." Drinking from the cup meant, "as I drink this wine, my life (my very blood) is yours, even if I must die to maintain this covenant relationship."

Finally, a memorial to the covenant agreement would be made by setting of stones or a tree being planted.

One of the most important concepts of the covenant was covenant partners actively seeking out and planning ways to fulfill the covenant. **Covenant partners constantly thought of ways to bless their covenant partner. This was not a passive agreement. Each tribe actively sought to help the other, always thinking and planning how to bless the other tribe. This was the desire of their hearts.**

In this way, the covenant partnership became the closest possible relationship. Covenant partners looked out for their partner's best interests. The covenant was proactive, not reactive. If someone robbed the Smith tribe, their covenant relationship tribe—the Jones tribe—would immediately act to right the wrong no matter how long it took or the cost. Nothing mattered except fulfilling their covenant relationship agreement. The ultimate insult to a covenant agreement was to think "Oh here they go again, getting in trouble and we have to bail them out." On the contrary, the thought would more likely be "Oh YES! They need us again to help them. This is what we live for, to help them be all they can be. We cannot wait to go out and fight, or even die, for them. This is what our life is all about."

In entering a covenant relationship, it was an honor to die fulfilling the covenant. It showed the purest heart of love by giving one's life to uphold the covenant relationship.

Entering a covenant is entering a relationship based on unconditional love, and only God is unconditional Love.

What is a Covenant Relationship with God?

God loves you more than you can ever conceive or know in your mind. Everything He does, all He allows into your path in life, has a specific purpose to transform you into His image, for you to become more One with Him. The purpose of everything that happens is for you to know Him better, to become more One with Him in body, mind, and spirit.

John 3:16-18

> *For God so loved the world, that he gave his only begotten Son, that whosoever believeth in him should not perish, but have everlasting life.*

> *For God sent not his Son into the world to condemn the world; but that the world through him might be saved.*

> *He that believeth on him is not condemned: but he that believeth not is condemned already* [because they have not entered the covenant relationship with God the Father through the covenant representative Jesus Christ], *because he hath not believed in the name of the only begotten Son of God.*

Jesus is the covenant representative of all humankind. He carries the covenant scars on His hands and feet. When one is "in Christ" they are One with the Father in Heaven and have eternal life not only when they die, but right at this moment as they live life to the fullest—fully experiencing His Love, His Joy, His Peace, and His Hope.

1 Cor 11:23-25

> *. . .that the Lord Jesus the same night in which he was be-trayed took bread:*
>
> *And when he had given thanks, he brake it, and said, Take, eat: this is my body* [this is the covenant meal, the Bread of Life], *which is broken for you: this do in remembrance of me* [when you eat of this Bread remember who you ARE IN CHRIST each moment. You are no longer controlled by the old nature, but now are under the control of Jesus Christ, being empowered by His Holy Spirit].
>
> *After the same manner also he took the cup, when he had supped, saying, this cup is the new testament in my blood* [this is the covenant drink, representing the new and ever-lasting covenant that was cut in His blood]: *this do ye, as oft as ye drink it, in remembrance of me* [remember who you ARE IN CHRIST].

As it was foretold many years before by the prophet Isaiah:

Isa 53:4-12

> *Surely he* [Jesus Christ, our covenant representative] *hath borne our griefs, and carried our sorrows* [upon Him was laid the price for all the past broken covenants with God]: *yet we did esteem him stricken, smitten of God, and afflict-ed.*
>
> *But he was wounded for our transgressions* [sally & george thoughts, words, and actions], *he was bruised for our iniq-uities: the chastisement of our peace was upon him* [all our sin, our sally & george nature, thoughts, and actions were laid upon Jesus so the debt was paid in full in His blood]; *and with his stripes we are healed* [in spirit, in soul, and in body].
>
> *All we like sheep have gone astray* [by following our sally

& george natures]; *we have turned everyone to his own way; and the* LORD *hath laid on him* [Jesus Christ, the sacrificial Lamb of God] *the iniquity* [penalty for following our sally & george natures] *of us all.*

He was oppressed, and he was afflicted, yet he opened not his mouth: he is brought as a lamb to the slaughter, and as a sheep before her shearers is dumb, so he openeth not his mouth [He came into the world for this purpose, to die a sacrificial death so that by His death He would set us free from the bondage satan, sally & george, and the world system had over us].

He was taken from prison and from judgment: and who shall declare his generation? for he was cut off out of the land of the living: for the transgression of my people was he stricken.

And he made his grave with the wicked, and with the rich in his death; because he had done no violence, neither was any deceit in his mouth [Jesus is perfect, He never gave into george].

Yet it pleased the LORD *to bruise him* [so you, His sons and His daughters, could be set free from the penalty of living life in bondage to sally & george, and from dying an eternal death separate from Him]; *he hath put him to grief: when thou shalt make his soul an offering for sin, he shall see his seed, he shall prolong his days, and the pleasure of the* LORD *shall prosper in his hand.*

He shall see of the travail of his soul, and shall be satisfied: by his knowledge shall my righteous servant justify many; for he shall bear their iniquities.

Therefore will I divide him a portion with the great, and he shall divide the spoil with the strong; because he hath poured out his soul unto death: and he was numbered with the transgressors; and he bare the sin of many, and made intercession for the transgressors.

To sum up, what covenant means is we have come back into a covenant relationship with our Father in Heaven because of what His Son and our LORD Jesus Christ, our covenant representative, did at the cross. When He died, He paid the price for all the broken covenants before this time, and cut a new, everlasting, and unbreakable covenant with His Father in Heaven. For you this means when you are "in Christ," in your new nature, you are perfect, and the Father sees you just as He sees His Son Jesus Christ.

This does not occur because of any good works you have done, or could ever do. It is based solely on what Jesus Christ did for you when He died and rose again. Any attempt to enter God our Father's presence apart from His Son's sacrifice is an abomination to God (this is the good works of door number 2). Jesus said "I am the Way, the Truth, and the Life: no man cometh unto the Father, but by Me." This means there is one, and only one, way to the Father. That way is through His appointed covenant representative Jesus Christ. No exceptions, no religions, no good works!

Old and New Covenants

The old covenant was a covenant of work. It was born in the tree of the knowledge of good and evil (doors 2 and 3). In other words, if you do good, you get good, and if you do bad, you get bad. An eye for an eye and a tooth for a tooth. This is the law of cause and effect, of sowing and reaping.

This covenant's first purpose was not to save the people, but to preserve them until the coming of the Messiah—Jesus Christ. The second purpose of this covenant was to show the people that no matter how hard they tried or how good they were, their actions were never good enough, were never up to God their Father in Heaven's standards, which are nothing short of perfection. It showed them they needed a Savior.

In the Old Testament, the differences can be seen in the following:

Ex 21:23-25

> *And if any mischief follow, then thou shalt give life for life,*
>
> *Eye for eye, tooth for tooth, hand for hand, foot for foot,*
>
> *Burning for burning, wound for wound, stripe for stripe.*

In the New Testament, Jesus said:

Matt 5:38-42

> *Ye have heard that it hath been said, An eye for an eye, and a tooth for a tooth:*
>
> *But I say unto you, That ye resist not evil* [a person filled with sally or george]*: but whosoever shall smite thee on thy right cheek, turn to him the other also.*
>
> *And if any man will sue thee at the law, and take away thy coat, let him have thy cloak also.*
>
> *And whosoever shall compel thee to go a mile, go with him twain* [two]*.*
>
> *Give to him that asketh thee, and from him that would borrow of thee turn not thou away.*

This cannot be done from the sally or george mind but must be done from the Christ-filled heart of Love and Truth spoken to you by the Holy Spirit.

Through Christ we have become a blessed people. What is this blessing?

In the Old Testament, the blessing was stated:

Gen 22:15-18

> *And the angel of the LORD called unto Abraham out of heaven the second time,*
>
> *And said, By myself have I sworn, saith the LORD, for be-*

cause thou hast done this thing, and hast not withheld thy son, thine only son:

That in blessing I will bless thee, and in multiplying I will multiply thy seed as the stars of the heaven, and as the sand which is upon the sea shore; and thy seed shall possess the gate of his enemies;

And in thy seed shall all the nations of the earth be blessed; because thou hast obeyed my voice [all nations will be blessed because of your obedience to Me].

In the New Testament, Paul restates the blessing:

Gal 3:16-29

Now to Abraham and his seed were the promises made. He saith not, And to seeds, as of many; but as of one, And to thy seed, which is Christ.

And this I say, that the covenant, that was confirmed before of God in Christ, the law [the law of sin and death], *which was four hundred and thirty years after, cannot disannul, that it should make the promise of none effect.*

For if the inheritance be of the law, it is no more of promise: but God gave it to Abraham by promise.

Wherefore then serveth the law? It was added because of transgressions, till the seed [Jesus Christ] *should come to whom the promise was made* [the purpose of the law was to preserve the nation until Jesus Christ was revealed and brought forth the new and everlasting covenant that was to be received by Grace, trusting in Jesus Christ, instead of by works of the law];

. . .for if there had been a law given which could have given life, verily righteousness should have been by the law.

But the scripture hath concluded all under sin [sally & george mind, will, desire, emotions, words, and actions], *that the promise by faith of Jesus Christ might be given to them that believe.*

But before faith* [trust] *came, we were kept under the law* [of sin and death], *shut up unto the faith which should afterwards be revealed.

***Wherefore the law* [the tree of the knowledge of good and evil] *was our schoolmaster to bring us unto Christ, that we might be justified by faith* [our trust in Jesus Christ, and Him alone].**

***But after that faith is come, we are no longer under a schoolmaster* [there is no more purpose for the law].**

For ye are all the children of God by faith in Christ Jesus.

For as many of you as have been baptized into Christ have put on Christ [you are in Christ in the new and everlasting covenant because you have trusted in the name of Jesus, your covenant representative between you and your Father in Heaven].

There is neither Jew nor Greek, there is neither bond nor free, there is neither male nor female: for ye are all one in Christ Jesus.

And if ye be Christ's, then are ye Abraham's seed, and heirs according to the promise.

God's Triple Assurance

God did something unprecedented. He made a promise to Abraham, this was enough. But then He made an oath in order to doubly secure that promise. He swore on Himself. But further, to make the promise absolutely secure for the doubting mind, He triply secured the promise by stating God cannot lie. Nothing is more secure than this in all of existence.

God's promise + God's oath + God cannot lie = permanent and eternal guarantee

God promises us the Holy Spirit directed life—eternal life in this moment. This Truth sets you free from the doubt and fear of the mind in this moment. He also promises us Heaven for eternity, as Jesus went to prepare a place for us. This is the anchor of our mind, our will, and our emotions: Heaven on earth (Truth being revealed in the moment) and Heaven as our home for eternity when our brief physical existence ends.

John 14:1-7

> *Let not your heart be troubled: ye believe in God, believe also in me.*
>
> *In my Father's house are many mansions: if it were not so, I would have told you. I go to prepare a place for you.*
>
> *And if I go and prepare a place for you, I will come again, and receive you unto myself; that where I am, there ye may be also* [this is our promise of eternal life in Heaven with Jesus].
>
> *And whither I go ye know, and the way ye know.*
>
> *Thomas saith unto him, Lord, we know not whither thou goest; and how can we know the way?*
>
> *Jesus saith unto him, I am the way, the truth, and the life: no man cometh unto the Father, but by me* [Jesus is the covenant representative between God the Father and fallen humanity. There is no way back to a relationship with God the Father except through Jesus Christ, who paid the price of all the old broken covenants and cut a new and everlasting covenant that could never be broken again].
>
> *If ye had known me, ye should have known my Father also: and from henceforth ye know him, and have seen him.*

Heb 6:13-20

> *For when God made promise to Abraham, because he could swear by no greater, he sware by himself,*
>
> *Saying, Surely blessing I will bless thee, and multiplying I will multiply thee.*
>
> *And so, after he had patiently endured, he obtained the promise.*
>
> *For men verily swear by the greater: and an oath for con-firmation is to them an end of all strife.*
>
> *Wherein God, willing more abundantly to shew unto the heirs of promise the immutability* [unchanging nature] *of his counsel, confirmed it by an oath:*
>
> *That by two immutable* [unchangeable] *things, in which it was impossible for God to lie, we might have a strong con-solation, who have fled for refuge to lay hold upon the hope set before us* [eternal life in Heaven with Jesus, and eternal life in the here and now with the Holy Spirit leading and directing our hearts]:
>
> *Which hope we have as an anchor of the soul, both sure and stedfast, and which entereth into that within the veil* [the hope of eternal life enters the Holy of Holies, which is in the presence of the Holy Spirit];
>
> *Whither the forerunner is for us entered, even Jesus, made an high priest for ever. . .*

Old Covenant Blessing

God's Spirit was with them, and blessings were seen primarily in prosperity. One example of needs being met physically is:

Deut 7:12-15

> *Wherefore it shall come to pass, if ye hearken to these judg-ments, and keep, and do them, that the LORD thy God shall*

keep unto thee the covenant and the mercy which he sware unto thy fathers:

And he will love thee, and bless thee, and multiply thee: he will also bless the fruit of thy womb, and the fruit of thy land, thy corn, and thy wine, and thine oil, the increase of thy kine, and the flocks of thy sheep, in the land which he sware unto thy fathers to give thee.

Thou shalt be blessed above all people: there shall not be male or female barren among you, or among your cattle.

And the LORD will take away from thee all sickness. . .

New Covenant Blessing

God's Spirit is within each person, within their heart. Blessings are seen in the mental/emotional and spiritual realms in freedom from adversity, allowing the death of the old nature. This blessing manifests in being content in every situation—I can do all things through Christ who strengthens me by the Power of the Holy Spirit within me.

Always be filled with Joy by being in the Holy Spirit, not by being in your sally or george mind.

Pray constantly and continually by being in constant communion with God the Father, and by listening to the Truth the Holy Spirit reveals to your heart in each of your life situations and circumstances.

Give thanks for each and every circumstance, because your Father in Heaven has a plan and purpose for all circumstances that come into your life—to transform you into the son or daughter of God He created you to be, to be Jesus on the planet.

This is God's will for you in Christ Jesus.

Do not quench the Holy Spirit's fire by following your old sally or george mind, apart from Christ. Instead, follow the Holy Spirit's direction and guidance with the Truth that will set you free each moment of your life.

You can see the new covenant blessing in Paul's life. He had learned the secret to contentment. It was found in the strength of the Holy Spirit which Jesus Christ provided.

Phil 4:11-13

> *Not that I speak in respect of want: for I have learned, in whatsoever state I am, therewith to be content.*

> *I know both how to* [live] *be abased* [in need]*, and I know how to* [live] *abound* [in abundance]*: every where and in all things I am instructed both to be full and to be hungry, both to abound and to suffer need.*

> *I can do all things through Christ which strengtheneth me* [by the power of the Holy Spirit within me, when I follow my Truth-filled heart in the moment, instead of my fact- and knowledge-filled mind].

Old Covenant Blessings	New Covenant Blessings
Covenant of keeping the law God commanded. By keeping the commandments, a relationship with God was maintained.	Covenant of the Grace, or gift of God. Eph 2:8-9 *For by grace are ye saved through faith; and that not of yourselves: it is the gift of God: Not of works, lest any man should boast.* Our relationship with God is maintained by trusting in what His Son, Jesus Christ, did, never by what we can or cannot do. If we even think about a sinful act, it is already counted as a sin against us. So the only way to maintain our relationship with the Father is through our covenant relationship with Jesus Christ, our covenant representative with the Father. To be "in Christ" is to be in what Jesus did rather than in what we can do. To be "in Christ" is to be in the covenant of Grace with the Father.

Physical blessings flow from obedience to the written law and the covenant with God. God was with them.	Physical, mental/emotional, and spiritual blessings flow from obeying the law of Love written on the heart. Knowing the covenant relationship with the Father is unbreakable, unlike past covenants, because this one was made between Jesus, the perfect God/Man, our covenant representative, and God the Father. When you are "in Christ" the Spirit of God is no longer with you but inside you, in your heart, directing and guiding you. The Holy Spirit gives you all Wisdom, Revelation, Truth, and Power on His timing with the sole purpose of glorifying the Father in Heaven.
Abundance of food.	My food is to do the will of the Father.
Abundance of crops and livestock.	Phil 4:19 *But my God shall supply all your need according to his riches in glory by Christ Jesus.* Phil 4:11-13 *Not that I speak in respect of want: for I have learned, in whatsoever state I am, therewith to be content.* *I know both how to [live] be abased [in need], and I know how to [live] abound [in abundance]: every where and in all things I am instructed both to be full and to be hungry, both to abound and to suffer need.* *I can do all things through Christ which strengtheneth me.*
Abundance of money.	Heb 13:5-6 *Let your conversation be without covetousness* [be free from the love of money and material possessions]*; and be content with such things as ye have: for he hath said, I will never leave thee, nor forsake thee.* *So that we may boldly say, The Lord is my helper, and I will not fear what man shall do unto me.*

Victory over enemies.	Eph 6:10-14 *Finally, my brethren, be strong in the Lord, and in the power of his might.* *Put on the whole armour of God, that ye may be able to stand against the wiles* [strategies] *of the devil.* *For we wrestle not against flesh and blood, but against principalities, against powers, against the rulers of the darkness of this world, against spiritual wickedness in high places* [in the spiritual realm]. *Wherefore take unto you the whole armour of God, that ye may be able to withstand in the evil day* [the moment the devil, demons, sallys or georges, or your own sally or george come against you], *and having done all, to stand.* *Stand therefore* [in who you ARE in Christ],. . . 1 Peter 5:8-10 *Be sober, be vigilant* [be awake, aware, and alert]; *because your adversary the devil, as a roaring lion, walketh about, seeking whom he may devour:* *Whom resist stedfast in the faith* [stand firm in your trust in Jesus, in what He did, said, and what He is doing right now], *knowing that the same afflictions are accomplished in your brethren that are in the world* [you are not the only one being tested]. *But the God of all grace, who hath called us unto his eternal glory by Christ Jesus, after that ye have suffered a while* [your sally or george has suffered], *make you perfect, stablish, strengthen, settle you* [the purpose of the test is to mature you in Christ Jesus, to strengthen you in the Power of the Holy Spirit working in your life, because when you are weak, He is strong].

Heb 12:1-5

. . .let us lay aside every weight, and the sin which doth so easily beset us [put aside the things of sally & george, and look at the weight not questioning whether you can lift it, but know the Holy Spirit will lift it through you. In doing so you will embrace your weakness, glorifying God], *and let us run with patience the race that is set before us* [be Patient and keep your eyes on Jesus—what He said, what He did, where He is right now, what He said you would do in His Name],

Looking unto Jesus the author and finisher of our faith; who for the joy that was set before him endured the cross, despising the shame, and is set down at the right hand of the throne of God.

For consider him that endured such contradiction of sinners against himself, lest ye be wearied and faint in your minds [do not grow tired of the journey and give up, retreating into your sally or george old mind].

Ye have not yet resisted unto blood, striving against sin [you have not yet resisted sally or george to the point of sweating blood as Jesus did].

And ye have forgotten the exhortation which speaketh unto you as unto children [remember above all else you are not alone, you are sons and daughters of God, you are covenant members of the Family of God],. . .

Being brought into the promised land.	**Gal 3:13-14** *Christ hath redeemed us from the curse of the law* [tree of the knowledge of good and evil, the law of sin and death, sally & george],. . . *That the blessing of Abraham might come on the Gentiles through Jesus Christ; that we might receive the promise of the* [Holy] *Spirit through faith* [trusting in Jesus Christ as our Lord and Savior, and trusting in His promise to send the Holy Spirit to live within us]. **John 8:31-36** *Then said Jesus to those Jews which believed on him, If ye continue in my word, then are ye my disciples indeed* [continue following His Word, living the Word from your heart, not just your good religious sally or george mind]; *And ye shall know the truth* [Jesus Christ]*, and the truth* [Jesus Christ] *shall make you free.* *They answered him, We be Abraham's seed, and were never in bondage to any man* [old covenant blessing]*: how sayest thou, Ye shall be made free?* *Jesus answered them, Verily, verily, I say unto you, Whosoever committeth sin is the servant of sin* [whoever follows the sally or george sin nature is a slave to sally or george]. . . . *If the Son therefore shall make you free* [from your sally or george nature, the world system of sallys and georges, along with the demons and devil]*, ye shall be free indeed.*

Abundance of physical possessions.	Matt 6:33-34 *But seek ye first the kingdom of God* [this translates from Aramaic to "counsel," so you are to seek the Counselor who is the Holy Spirit], *and his righteousness* [this is your right standing with God when you are in the new and everlasting covenant with your Father in Heaven through the covenant representative Jesus Christ. When you are IN CHRIST you are the righteousness of Jesus Christ]*; and all these things shall be added unto you.* *Take therefore no thought for the morrow: for the morrow shall take thought for the things of itself. Sufficient unto the day is the evil thereof* [do not dwell on tomorrow, or even later today, because the future and past are strongholds of sally & george. Instead, live fully in the moment, keeping your eyes on Jesus and letting the Holy Spirit's Truth and Power flow through the weakness of your old nature].
Keeping the Sabbath day.	Heb 4:9-10 *There remaineth therefore a rest* [Sabbath] *to the people of God* [resting from trying to please God with their good, religious sally & george acts, instead resting in the finished WORK of Jesus Christ, resting IN HIM in the new covenant of Grace and the Truth He speaks to the heart]. *For he that is entered into his rest, he also hath ceased from his own works, as God did from his.*

Disease free —will not get cancer.	Freedom from disease and the fear of all disease— the Calm in the midst of the storm. If you let sally or george take so much control over your body and mind that diseases like cancer form, then the Holy Spirit will reveal the Truth in the situation, and the Truth will set you free from the fear of the cancer. Whether the cancer leaves or stays does not matter (although when you are fully IN CHRIST, it will go, because Jesus cannot have cancer, so you cannot have cancer when you are fully IN CHRIST). You have gone to the place of freedom from all "things," freedom from all physical, both good or bad. What the world system, satan, sallys and georges of the world, and your own sally or george mean to harm you, God means for Good. No matter how powerfully you are hit by these forces, as long as you follow the Truth God speaks to your heart, without trying to save yourself, these situations will be the weakness where His Truth and Power manifest in your life. The end result is always Victory and Freedom.
The law of sowing and reaping manifested in physical form.	Christ is all and in all. Jesus is the first, the last, and everything in between. We sow our life, our body, our mind, our heart, and our soul to Christ and we reap the Grace of God. When we sow the death of our sally or george mind, we reap eternal life in the moment—Truth sets us free from the lie of the old sally or george mind.

The law of cause and effect manifested in physical form.	Col 1:15-17 *Who is the image of the invisible God, the first-born of every creature:* *For by him were all things created, that are in heaven, and that are in earth, visible and invisible, whether they be thrones, or dominions, or principalities, or powers: all things were created by him, and for him:* *And he is before all things, and by him all things consist.* Col 3:11 *. . .Christ is all, and in all.* Once you come to Him, He is the cause and effect of everything in your life. There is no more cause and effect, no more happy and sad, no more good and bad unless you choose to go back and live in your old nature apart from Christ in that moment. Once you separate from Christ in the moment, you are again in the old mind of sally or george, and you are under the law of cause and effect, the law of sin and death, instead of being under the Law of the Spirit of Life being "in Christ."

What is the blessing of Abraham?

Gal 3:14

> *That the blessing of Abraham might come on the Gentiles through Jesus Christ; that we might receive the promise of the* [Holy] *Spirit through faith* [trusting in Jesus Christ as our Lord and Savior, and trusting in His promise to send the Holy Spirit to live within us].

The blessing of Abraham was God's promise to send His Son to be the new covenant representative, and through His Son, all who called on the name of Jesus Christ would be saved, set free, delivered, made whole, healed in body, mind, and spirit. The physical manifestation of the blessing of Abraham in the New Testament was the Holy Spirit of

Truth and Power living within the person. Now God would no longer just walk alongside you, but His Spirit would live inside of you, in your heart, always leading and guiding you into all Truth, into all Jesus said.

Eph 1:13-14

> *In whom ye also trusted* [when you trusted in Jesus Christ as your Lord and Savior], *after that ye heard the word of truth, the gospel of your salvation: in whom also after that ye believed, ye were sealed with that holy Spirit of promise,*
>
> *Which is the earnest* [assured deposit] *of our inheritance until the redemption of the purchased possession, unto the praise of his glory.*

Would you rather have Jesus walking with you, or have His Holy Spirit living inside of you every hour of every day, all year long? Jesus said it was best for Him to go, so the Holy Spirit could come and live within us.

John 16:7

> *Nevertheless I tell you the truth; It is expedient* [far better] *for you that I go away: for if I go not away, the Comforter* [the Holy Spirit] *will not come unto you; but if I depart, I will send him unto you.*

Eph 1:3

> *Blessed be the God and Father of our Lord Jesus Christ, who hath blessed us with all spiritual blessings* [the man-ifestation of the blessings of the Holy Spirit in your life when you are fully in Christ in the moment] *in heavenly places in Christ:*

Remember, this blessing is dependent upon being "in Christ" in each and every moment, and not merely a one-time decision to follow Him. You can be a follower of Christ, yet not be "in Him" in this very moment. In that moment, you are in sally or george. Living in sally or george is living a life of defeat and bondage, because although you know Him and love Him, you are not actively choosing Him that very moment, you are not fixing your eyes on Jesus that moment. If you are not "in Christ" in this moment, then you are surely in your old sally or george nature. You have two choices: choose Christ, or choose sally or george. If you do not actively choose to be "in Christ," you default to sally or george.

James 1:12

> *Blessed is the man that endureth temptation* [passed the test by staying "in Christ," and at the same time staying in the weakness, suffering sally or george by obeying the Truth that the Holy Spirit reveals, instead of letting the sally or george mind take control of the situation in an attempt to remove the suffering]: *for when he is tried, he shall receive the crown of life* [this is eternal life, forever and also in the moment. This is the Truth that sets you free, the Power to overcome all things. This is the Love, Joy, Peace, and Hope that only the Holy Spirit can give. This is His kingdom come, His will be done, on earth as it is done in Heaven], *which the Lord hath promised to them that love him* [who have entered into a blood covenant relationship with Him through His covenant representative Jesus Christ].

1 Peter 4:12-14

> *Beloved, think it not strange concerning the fiery trial which is to try you, as though some strange thing happened unto you:*
>
> *But rejoice, inasmuch as ye are partakers of Christ's sufferings* [suffering sally & george, putting the old sally or george mind, will, desire, emotions, and thoughts to death along with separating from the world system ruled by sallys and georges]; *that, when his glory shall be revealed, ye*

may be glad also with exceeding joy.

If ye be reproached [attacked or condemned] *for the name of Christ* [to choose Jesus' name is to choose death to the sally or george nature, and sally & george do not die easily], *happy are ye* [you will be filled with the Joy of the Holy Spirit]; *for the spirit of glory and of God resteth upon you* [the Holy Spirit is powerfully manifesting through your acceptance of the weakness of sally or george, and your staying in that weakness so His Power can be made perfect]:. . .

Matt 5:3-12

Blessed are the poor in spirit [those who trust only in what Christ and the Holy Spirit speak to their hearts, and not what sally or george and the world system speak to their minds]: *for theirs is the kingdom of heaven.*

Blessed are they that mourn [this comes from putting sally or george to death moment by moment, by staying in their weakness, and suffering sally or george, not trying to get out of the suffering]: *for they shall be comforted* [by the Holy Spirit who brings Love, Joy, Peace, Hope, and Truth into the heart].

Blessed are the meek [those who do not boast in sally or george, but rest in what IS because He is always with them; rest in the moment that their Father in Heaven has allowed for their growth and transformation]: *for they shall inherit the earth.*

Blessed are they which do hunger and thirst after righteousness [Jesus is the only true righteousness, and knowing that Christ is all, and in all]: *for they shall be filled.*

Blessed are the merciful: for they shall obtain mercy.

Blessed are the pure in heart [those with Christ in their heart, separated from sally or george and the world system run by sallys and georges, each and every moment]: *for they shall see God.*

Blessed are the peacemakers [those who follow the Peace that the Holy Spirit fills their heart with, not those who try to make peace in the world. Jesus said He did not come to make peace, but division; dividing heart and mind]: *for they shall be called the children of God.*

Blessed are they which are persecuted for righteousness' sake [because of choosing Jesus, who is God of the moment, instead of choosing sally or george and the world system every moment]: *for theirs is the kingdom of heaven.*

Blessed are ye, when men shall revile you, and persecute you, and shall say all manner of evil against you falsely [because they are in their sally or george nature, being ruled by their minds, while you are in Christ, being ruled by your Truth-filled heart], *for my sake.*

Rejoice, and be exceeding glad: for great is your reward in heaven: for so persecuted they the prophets which were before you.

This blessing of Abraham is to know Jesus Christ as Lord and Savior, and to have His Holy Spirit live within your heart, bringing forth the blessing that all your sally or george actions and thoughts are covered by the blood of Jesus. God your Father in Heaven no longer sees your sally or george nature. He only sees your Christ-like nature.

Rom 4:4-8

Now to him that worketh is the reward not reckoned of grace [if you work for something, it is not a gift, but rather a reward for your work], *but of debt.*

But to him that worketh not, but believeth on him that justifieth the ungodly, his faith is counted for righteousness [right standing with the Father in Heaven through the new covenant representative, Jesus Christ].

Even as David also describeth the blessedness of the man, unto whom God imputeth [gives, imparts] *righteousness without works,*

Saying, Blessed are they whose iniquities [sins—sally & george thoughts, words, and actions] *are forgiven, and whose sins are covered.*

Blessed is the man to whom the Lord will not impute sin [sally or george thoughts, desires, words, and actions are not held against him because the Father sees that man as He sees His Son Jesus Christ—perfect and without sin].

3

YOU CANNOT MIX THE OLD COVENANT WITH THE NEW COVENANT

One of the most powerful tactics of sally & george is to mix the Tree of Life with the tree of the knowledge of good and evil, to mix Grace with the law and good works, to mix the Truth-filled heart with the fact- and knowledge-filled mind, to mix the new covenant with the old covenant.

A dilemma arises when one enters the new covenant relationship with the Father in Heaven through His Son and our covenant representative, Jesus Christ, yet still tries to follow old covenant laws and principles.

To live from a heart of Truth, you cannot also live from a mind of knowledge.

To live empowered by the Holy Spirit of God, you cannot also live comfortably and safely from the strength of the mind.

To live from the Tree of Life—having eternal life (the Spirit of God, fully in each moment), you cannot also live from the tree of the knowledge of good and evil, trying to have good moments.

To live by the Law of the Spirit of Life, you cannot also live by the law of sin and death.

To live by the Grace of God (what Jesus did for you at the cross when He died to pay the price for all past broken covenants and then shed His blood to cut the new and everlasting covenant of Grace), you cannot live by any works, actions, laws, or principles based on cause and effect or sowing and reaping. You cannot mix the two. You live either by Grace, or by works and law. You either accept the gift freely, or believe you are receiving a reward for your actions.

You cannot receive the gift then come back and say, "I would like to pay you something for it." Doing so not only nullifies the gift, but also insults the giver of the gift.

You cannot mix the old covenant with the new covenant! You cannot mix law with Grace!

Luke 5:36-38

> *And he spake also a parable unto them; No man putteth a piece of a new garment upon an old; if otherwise, then both the new maketh a rent* [tear], *and the piece that was taken out of the new agreeth not* [will not look like] *with the old.*

> *And no man putteth new wine into old bottles; else the new wine will burst the bottles, and be spilled, and the bottles shall perish.*

> *But new wine must be put into new bottles. . .*

Gal 3:6-14

> *Even as Abraham believed God, and it was accounted to him for righteousness.*

> *Know ye therefore that they which are of faith* [trusting in Jesus Christ as their Lord and Savior], *the same are the children of Abraham.*

> *And the scripture, foreseeing that God would justify the heathen* [non-Jew] *through faith, preached before the gospel unto Abraham, saying, In thee shall all nations be blessed.*

> *So then they which be of faith* [in Jesus Christ] *are blessed with faithful Abraham.*

For as many as are of the works of the law are under the curse [those who rely on keeping the commandments for their righteousness]*: for it is written, Cursed is every one that continueth not in all things which are written in the book of the law to do them* [Jesus said that merely thinking about breaking a commandment means it has been broken, so no one can keep them, apart from being in a covenant relationship with Him].

But that no man is justified by the law in the sight of God, it is evident: for, The just shall live by faith [by trusting in the new covenant of Grace that comes by being "in Christ"].

And the law is not of faith: but, The man that doeth them shall live in them.

Christ hath redeemed us from the curse of the law, being made a curse for us: for it is written, Cursed is every one that hangeth on a tree:

That the blessing of Abraham might come on the Gentiles through Jesus Christ; that we might receive the promise of the Spirit [the Holy Spirit of Truth and Power living within you] *through faith* [trusting in God the Father, Jesus Christ, and the Holy Spirit].

Gal 3:23-29

But before faith came, we were kept under the law [by religious sally or george living from the good side of the tree of knowledge, door number 2], *shut up unto the faith* [trusting in Jesus Christ, the new covenant representative] *which should afterwards be revealed.*

Wherefore the law [which fed the sally & george religion-filled minds] ***was our schoolmaster to bring us unto Christ, that we might be justified by faith*** [by trusting in Jesus and Jesus alone for everything].

But after that faith is come, we are no longer under a

schoolmaster **[the power of the religion-filled, good works, good actions, and good words of the sally & george nature]**.

For ye are all the children [sons and daughters] *of God by faith* [trusting] *in Christ Jesus* [what Jesus did at the cross].

For as many of you as have been baptized [submerged] *into Christ have put on Christ* [to be clothed in Christ is like putting on a Jesus suit, you now look like, talk, and act just like Jesus].

. . .

And if ye be Christ's, then are ye Abraham's seed, and heirs according to the promise [the new covenant of Grace, being filled with and led by the Holy Spirit of Truth].

Heb 8:7-13

For if that first covenant had been faultless, then should no place have been sought for the second.

For finding fault with them, he saith, *Behold, the days come, saith the Lord, when I will make a new covenant with the house of Israel and with the house of Judah:*

Not according to the covenant that I made with their fathers in the day when I took them by the hand to lead them out of the land of Egypt; because they continued not in my covenant, and I regarded them not, saith the Lord.

For this is the covenant that I will make with the house of Israel after those days, saith the Lord; I will <u>put my laws</u> into their mind, and <u>write them in their hearts</u>: and I will be to them a God, and they shall be to me a people:

And they shall not teach every man his neighbor, and every man his brother, saying, Know the Lord: for all shall know me, from the least to the greatest.

For I will be merciful [forgiving] *to their unrighteous-*

ness, and their sins and their iniquities will I remember no more.

In that he saith, A new covenant, he hath made the first old [the old covenant was meant to vanish or disappear]. *Now that which decayeth and waxeth old is ready to vanish away.*

Heb 9:15

And for this cause he [Jesus Christ] *is the mediator* [covenant representative] *of the new testament* [covenant], *that by means of* [Jesus'] *death, for the redemption of the transgressions that were under the first testament* [paid the price to set us free from the law of sin and death under the old covenant], *they which are called might receive the promise of eternal inheritance* [in Christ, with the presence of the Holy Spirit living within you].

Heb 10:15-19

Whereof the Holy [Spirit of Truth] *Ghost also is a witness to us: for after that he had said before,*

This is the covenant that I will make with them after those days, saith the Lord, **I will put my laws into their hearts,** *and in their minds will I write them;*

And their sins [sally or george thoughts, words, and actions] *and iniquities will I remember no more.*

Now where remission of these is, there is no more offering for sin.

Having therefore, brethren [we have the], *boldness* [confidence, assurance, because we are now members of the Family of God through Christ Jesus] *to enter into the holiest by the blood of Jesus* [to enter into the Holy of Holies, which is the very presence of God in the Holy Spirit, we can run right into the throne room of God our Father because of the blood of the new and everlasting covenant cut by our covenant representative Jesus Christ],

Is living by Grace alone giving one an open door to sin?

Some will say that if a person lives by Grace and Grace alone, without any punishment for their sins, they are given an open door to sin. They say one must balance Grace with the law, otherwise a person will sin without repentance, and sin more freely without punishment or a price to pay for their sin, for living in the desires of sally or george.

No one would sensibly want to live in her or his sally or george nature, apart from God, once they have entered into the new blood covenant relationship with God their Father through their most precious covenant representative Jesus Christ. Once you have experienced true Love in your heart, that Love compels you. If you are truly in love with your spouse, do you need to follow 500 commandments of what not to do in marriage, or do you follow the one command of Love which rules your heart? True Love drives you to make the object of your love all he or she is created to be. True Love is not self-seeking, never thinks of self at all, because true Love is too busy focusing 100% of their energy on their covenant partner, waiting on the Holy Spirit of Truth to reveal how to bless and give them more, and help them be all their Father in Heaven created them to be.

Once you enter the covenant relationship with Jesus Christ, you understand the words "Christ, who is our life" and "Christ is all and in all." When you have been given everything God has created for you so you can be all He created you to be, you don't go looking for something else.

Rom 5:20-6:10

> *Moreover the law entered* [the tree of the knowledge of good and evil, the law of sin and death], *that the offence* [your sally or george nature, thoughts, words, and actions] *might abound. But where sin* [sally & george thoughts,

words, and actions] *abounded, grace* [the gift of eternal life that comes through Jesus Christ alone] *did much more abound:*

That as sin hath reigned unto death, even so might grace reign through righteousness [your right standing in God's presence only comes through your covenant representative Jesus Christ and being "in Christ" in all that He did, rather than trying to be in what you can do] *unto eternal life by Jesus Christ our Lord.*

What shall we say then? Shall we continue in sin, that grace may abound?

God forbid. How shall we, that are dead to sin [sally & george are no longer sitting on the throne of your life], live any longer therein?

Know ye not, that so many of us as were baptized [submerged] *into Jesus Christ were baptized* [submerged] *into his death?*

Therefore we are buried with him by baptism into death: that like as Christ was raised up from the dead by the glory of the Father, even so we also should walk in newness of life [resurrection life, eternal life].

For if we have been planted together in the likeness of his death, we shall be also in the likeness of his resurrection:

Knowing this, that our old man [sally & george nature, thoughts, words, and actions] *is crucified with him* [sally & george have been nailed to the cross], *that the body of sin might be destroyed* [sally's or george's power over you has been destroyed by Jesus Christ], *that henceforth we should not serve sin* **[we no longer have to let sally or george run our life. WE NO LONGER HAVE TO SIN]**.

For he who is dead [to sally or george controlling your life] *is freed from sin.*

Now if we be dead with Christ, we believe we shall also live with him [eternally in Heaven and bringing Heaven to earth, eternal life in this moment by waiting for the Holy Spirit to reveal the Truth in the moment which sets us free from the doubt and fear of the mind].

Knowing that Christ being raised from the dead dieth no more [cannot die anymore]; *death hath no more dominion* [power] *over him.*

For in that he died, he died unto sin once [to pay the price of all sin]: *but in that he liveth, he liveth unto* [He lives to the glory of] *God.*

Rom 6:11-23

Likewise reckon ye also yourselves to be dead indeed unto sin [sally & george have no more power over you], *but alive unto God through Jesus Christ our Lord.*

Let not sin [sally or george thoughts, words, or actions] *therefore reign in your mortal body, that ye should obey it in the lusts thereof.*

Neither yield ye your members as instruments of unrighteousness unto sin: but yield yourselves unto God [by obeying His Holy Spirit speaking to your heart], *as those that are alive from the dead, and your members as instruments of righteousness unto God.*

For sin shall not have dominion over you: for ye are not under the law [of sin and death], *but under grace* [the Law of the Spirit of Life].

What then? shall we sin, because we are not under the law, but under grace? God forbid.

Know ye not, that to whom ye yield yourselves servants to obey, his servants ye are to whom ye obey; whether of sin unto death [slaves to the control of the sally or george mind, will, and emotions], *or of obedience* [to the Holy Spirit revealing Truth to your heart] *unto righteousness?*

But God be thanked, that ye were the servants of sin [sally & george thoughts, words, and actions], *but ye have obeyed from the heart that form of doctrine which was delivered you.*

Being then made free from sin, ye became the servants of righteousness [to Jesus Christ and the Power of the Holy Spirit of Truth].

I speak after the manner of men because of the infirmity [weakness] *of your flesh* [in sally or george]: *for as ye have yielded your members servants to uncleanness and to iniquity unto iniquity; even so now yield your members servants to righteousness unto holiness.*

For when ye were the servants of sin [sally or george], *ye were free from righteousness* [because sally or george ruled you, you could not hear the Holy Spirit revealing the Truth to your heart].

What fruit had ye then in those things whereof ye are now ashamed? for the end of those things is death.

But now being made free from sin, and become servants to God, ye have your fruit unto holiness [the Holy Spirit-directed life], ***and the end everlasting life*** [the Truth which is revealed to set you free in the moment].

For the wages of sin [living from sally or george] ***is death; but the gift of God is eternal life*** [receiving and living from the Holy Spirit of Truth each moment] ***through Jesus Christ our Lord.***

Three levels of maturity exist in the Christian Life

1 John 2:12-14

> *I write unto you, little children, because your sins are for-given you for his name's sake.*
>
> *I write unto you, fathers, because ye have known him that is from the beginning. I write unto you, young men, because ye have overcome the wicked one. I write unto you, little children, because ye have known the Father.*
>
> *I have written unto you, fathers, because ye have known him that is from the beginning. I have written unto you, young men, because ye are strong, and the word of God abideth* [lives and dwells] *in you, and ye have overcome the wicked one.*

The three levels of your Christian maturity are:
1. **Children**—law
2. **Young men**—law + Grace
3. **Fathers**—Grace

Children are just that, babies in the journey. They have needs and wants they bring before their Father in Heaven. Their focus is on themselves, and they seek the Father in prayer to make things better for themselves. Babies and young children need the law to keep them from harming themselves. Parents tell their children what to do or not do because they have to protect them. The law is necessary for babies and young children because they have not yet matured; they don't know better. Their prayer would be "Father, heal me!"

Young men (and women) have matured past this total focus on self. Seeing what the world is really about, they begin to see the duality in existence—God and satan, angels and demons, their new nature "in Christ" and their old nature (sally or george) apart from Christ. They see the battle is against the devil, demons, and the sally or george nature and those lies trying to block the Truth of the Holy Spirit from setting them free in each moment. At this point, the law begins to transform into Grace. This person is starting to experience the Grace of God and is starting to see beyond the laws they were trained under as a young child of God. Their prayer would be "thank you Father for healing me 2,000 years ago in Jesus Christ."

Fathers (and mothers) have become all their Heavenly Father created them to be. They have transformed into the image and likeness of God's Son, Jesus Christ. At this level, they no longer see themselves. Rather, they see God's hand in everything. Everything in their life is about Him. The duality attained at the "young men" level has now transformed back to "God is One." At this level, their total focus is on God, and the self, the "I, me, my, mine," has faded away. When one matures to the father/mother level, they have become so like Christ that their total existence is consumed with the desire to know the Father better and to only glorify Him, to only do His will in their life.

At this level of maturity, the law has disappeared and only Grace exists. Life is filled with waiting for the Truth the Holy Spirit reveals each moment to once again set the person free from the lie of the old mind. The words "Christ is all and in all" becomes Truth in their heart, not just good words in their mind. Spiritual fathers/mothers know the Father, the Son, and the Holy Spirit and see them working in every area of life. satan, sally & george, the sallys & georges of the world, the world system, doubt, fear, time, and physicality no longer matter. All that counts is as spoken by Paul:

Col 3:1-4

> *If ye then be risen with Christ, seek those things which are above, where Christ sitteth on the right hand of God.*
>
> *Set your affection* [mind and thoughts] *on things above, not on things on the earth* [of the world].
>
> **For ye are dead [when you entered the covenant relationship with Jesus Christ, your sally or george nature died in the sense of no longer controlling you],** *and your life is hid with Christ in God.*

When Christ, who is our life, shall appear, then shall ye also appear with him in glory.

2 Cor 13:14

The grace of the Lord Jesus Christ, and the love of God, and the communion [intimate relationship or fellowship] *of the Holy* [Spirit] *Ghost, be with you all. Amen.*

Phil 3:8-11

...I count all things but loss for the excellency of the knowledge of Christ Jesus my Lord: for whom I have suffered the loss of all things, and do count them but dung, that I may win [be fully in] *Christ,*

And be found in him, not having mine own righteousness, which is of the law [being in the good, religious sally or george], *but that which is through the faith of Christ, the righteousness which is of God by faith:*

That I may know him [know Jesus Christ as a blood covenant Brother and as an intimate marriage Partner, the two becoming One], *and the power of his resurrection* **[eternal life in the here and now],** *and the fellowship of his sufferings, being made conformable unto his death* **[putting the sally or george nature to death by keeping him or her nailed to the cross each moment];**

If by any means I might attain unto the resurrection of the dead.

Prayer at the father (mother) level would not be about self at all. Fathers (mothers) do not ask for healing or thank Him for their healing. Instead, they fall to the floor and worship the Lord in praise and thanksgiving for who He IS!

Rev 7:11-12

> *And all the angels stood round about the throne, and about the elders and the four beasts, and fell before the throne on their faces, and worshipped God,*
>
> *Saying, Amen: Blessing, and glory, and wisdom, and thanksgiving, and honor, and power, and might, be unto our God for ever and ever. Amen.*

These three levels of spiritual maturity are not dependent upon how hard you work (law). Rather they come as God reveals them to you in your life journey (Grace). Praying harder or reading your Bible more will not raise you from a child to a father or mother. Maturity comes in God's time, not yours.

Your job is to seek Truth in every situation in your life and, no matter how long it takes, wait for the Holy Spirit to reveal the Truth which will set you free from the lie of the mind. Your job is to separate from the sally or george lies and the fact-filled mind as you seek the Truth which will set you free. Most importantly, your job is to remain in the weakness of sally or george, in the pain of not letting sally or george take control (this is suffering sally or george), and letting the Holy Spirit of Truth and Power manifest in that weakness.

So, does Grace need the law to keep it balanced?

To finally resolve the question of the necessity of the law to balance Grace, lest you live a life of sin without punishment, all we must do is look to the lives of Job and Noah, who lived over a thousand years before Moses and before the law was ever given.

Job 1:1

> *There was a man in the land of Uz, whose name was Job; and that man was perfect and upright* [righteous]*, and one that feared God, and eschewed* [separated from] *evil.*

Gen 6:8-9

> *But Noah found grace in the eyes of the Lord.*
>
> *. . .Noah was a just* [righteous] *man and perfect in his gen-erations, and Noah walked with God.*

The most important point about Job and Noah is they were perfect and righteous men, meaning they were in right standing with God. The Bible does not say they were sinless or guiltless, but in their hearts they knew they were right with God. How did such perfection and righteousness come to Job and Noah? Well, for one thing, it did not come by keeping the law, because Job and Noah lived long before Moses and long before there was any law.

That leaves one explanation. Job and Noah were perfect because God revealed His righteousness to them, He placed it in their hearts and in their minds. Their perfection was not based on good works but on the love of God they felt in their hearts. When a parent loves a child so much, the child feels that love and knows they are perfect in their parent's eyes. This great love frees the child to be the perfection that their parent sees in them. This is how it was with Job and Noah. The word says Job had a reverence for God, and he shunned evil, meaning he knew in his heart which actions were wrong, and he did not give in to them. Noah walked with God, meaning Noah had a relationship with God. He knew God in his heart, and listened to the Truth the Holy Spirit spoke to his heart. Both these men were righteous in God's eyes, and both men had a pure heart filled with the Spirit of God.

This is the design your Father in Heaven has for your life. The law preserved the nation until Jesus came, and the law showed that you could never hold to the law, and needed a Savior. Once Jesus came and gave us the Holy Spirit, we no longer needed the law, as the new Law of the Spirit of Life was written upon our hearts. No longer would we have the old law of sin and death written upon our minds. If Job and Noah lived righteous, perfect, Godly lives purely through the Grace of God and His Holy Spirit filling their hearts with Truth, so can you live a life by Grace without any need for the law to balance the Grace. The old has gone, and the new has come.

Grace in Action

If Grace is Jesus and the gift of salvation He alone can give, and works are your actions and words, let's look at the formula:

From the Grace of Jesus Christ flow the actions and Word of the Holy Spirit.

From the gift of salvation of body, mind, and spirit Jesus Christ gives, flows the Truth and Power of the Holy Spirit into your heart. This Truth and Power then brings forth God's will in your life, God's actions through your body, and God's Word from your mouth.

This is how Laurie (my covenant partner for eternity) was healed. In seeking Him and His Holy Spirit of Truth to reveal God's will for her journey into disease, the Holy Spirit revealed Seven Basic Steps to Total Health. These steps are:

- Air
- Water
- Food
- Sleep
- Exercise
- Fasting/Detoxification
- Prayer/Meditation/Stillness

Through these Seven Basic Steps came her healing. Did these Seven Basic Steps actually heal her? Absolutely not! Jesus Christ healed her, but His methods for healing, spoken into our hearts, were these Seven Basic Steps.

Through obeying what the Holy Spirit spoke to her heart, the love of my life followed the Seven Basic Steps to Total Health, and her healing came.

Your sally or george mind will try to steal God's glory by saying "Look how these Seven Basic Steps healed you. Make sure you never break them, or your healing will leave. Focus your energy to always keep these Seven Basic Steps in order to remain healthy. If you do not, your sickness will return."

Do you see the lie of the sally or george mind?

Do you recognize how they twist the Truth to keep you in bondage to them, how they keep themselves on the throne of your life?

To explain this great deception of sally & george, let us remember how Jesus healed those who came to Him for healing. For some, He laid His hands on them, and they were healed. For others, He spoke the Word, and they were healed. For others, He said to show themselves to the priest, and they were healed as they went. And for yet others, He rubbed mud on their eyes and told them to wash in a specific pool, and they were healed.

The question is this: Did the mud heal them? Did walking toward the priests heal them? No, Jesus healed them through different actions and acts of obedience to His Word. So what does the sally or george religion-filled mind say to do? Worship the mud, worship the pool they washed in, worship the path they walked on their way to the priests.

Jesus Christ, and Jesus alone, is the Healer.

Are you starting to get the big picture? Your everything, your life, your breath, your meaning for existence, your healing, your wholeness, all come from Jesus and Jesus alone. He might use different avenues for the healing to flow, but only the Healer is to be worshipped, not the avenue.

Through the Grace of Jesus Christ came the action of the Seven Basic Steps to Total Health, the vehicle He used to deliver His healing.

In Summary

You have two natures if you have entered the new and everlasting covenant with God your Father in Heaven through the atoning sacrifice of Jesus Christ, your Lord and Savior. Your new nature in Christ is your perfect God nature which makes you a son or daughter of God. Your new nature adopts you into the Family of God, making you an heir along with Christ. This nature is led and empowered by the Holy Spirit of God. Your new nature must be actively chosen through your free will each moment, so the blessing of Abraham, which is the Holy Spirit, can flow through your thoughts, actions, and words each and every moment.

If you choose Jesus Christ to be your Lord and Savior at only one point in time, but the rest of your life you live by trying to do the best you can, although you are in the Family of God and will go to Heaven after you die, your life on this planet will be less than He meant it to be for you.

You will live in defeat, not in Victory and Freedom. You will live a life guided by your old nature, even though you have a new nature. You will be living from the happy/sad, good/bad tree of the knowledge of good and evil and miss out on living your true potential moment by moment in the Tree of Life, in the Holy Spirit, being "in Christ" each and every moment.

God your Father in Heaven has given you free will to choose life or death, blessing or curse, not just once but each moment of your life. You are called to choose eternal life (to be in Christ, empowered by the Holy Spirit) each moment, because if you do not, you will be choosing to be in the good and bad, happy and sad, sally & george nature. As Jesus said, "he that is not with me is against me."

We urge you right now to be all God created you to be by choosing to be "in Christ" each moment of your life, instead of letting the good and bad mind, will, and emotions rule you. When you choose Him each moment, you will live an eternal life on planet earth before you enter Heaven. You will fulfill Jesus' command:

John 14:12-13

> *Verily, verily, I say unto you* [Jesus is saying "I am telling you the Truth, I am telling you the Truth." Everything Jesus said was Truth, but here He is emphasizing the importance of this statement through repetition], *He that believeth on me* [if you have entered a covenant relationship with Me and trust Me with all your heart, soul, mind, and strength], *the works that I do shall he do also; and greater works than these shall he do* [you will say and do everything I said and did, and even more than I did, because you are in the Family of God, as I AM, and you will do what your Family does, being empowered by the Holy Spirit]; *because I go unto my Father.*
>
> *And whatsoever ye shall ask in my name* [asking in Jesus' name means asking as a blood covenant brother, as an in-

timate marriage partner, when the two have become One],
that will I do, that the Father may be glorified in the Son
[I will answer your prayer if it is prayer from a member of
the Family of God, bringing glory to the Father in Heaven].

What this means is Jesus is now at the right hand of the Father interceding for you, and He has placed His Holy Spirit inside your heart.
You cannot fail to do as He did with the Holy Spirit flowing in and
through you, as He did in and through Jesus. Further, you have the
added benefit of Jesus praying for you constantly, and never did one
of Jesus' prayers to the Father go unanswered. The only way to fail
in this perfect plan is to fail to choose to be "in Christ" each moment,
so choosing indirectly to live from your good and bad, happy and sad,
sally or george nature, mind, will, and emotions, apart from Christ. The
defeated life so many live grieves our Father in Heaven, our Lord Jesus
Christ, and the Holy Spirit who lives within us. This does not have to
be. A better way is available.

The better way is to fix your thoughts and your mind on Jesus. Constantly remember He died so you could live an eternal life in the here
and now, empowered by the Holy Spirit, as well as an eternal life forever in Heaven with Him.

How do you live this impossible life? By never forgetting what Jesus
did and said for you 2,000 years ago, and by knowing what your future
holds. Remembering this will anchor you in the moment with the Holy
Spirit. Do not ever forget the anchor of your soul (your mind, your will,
and your emotions) is the Hope of Jesus preparing a place for you in
Heaven, that He would send His Holy Spirit to live within your heart
after He went to Heaven, and that the Holy Spirit would reveal all Truth
to set you free from the fear and doubt sally & george bring each moment.

The Holy Spirit will remind you of everything Jesus said when you
need reminding (when sally or george seem to be winning the battle of
the moment). The Holy Spirit will empower you to do the things your
sally or george mind says you cannot, though He spoke them into your
heart. The Holy Spirit will give you the Love, Joy, Peace, and Hope;
the Calm in the midst of any storm of the mind or world system. The

Holy Spirit of Power will enable you to take captive every thought of sally or george and make her or him obedient to Christ, meaning to keep every thought focused on Christ, on what He said, what He did, where He is, where you will be, and what He is doing right now, which is praying for you to stay in your Holy Spirit-filled heart.

Heb 3:1

Wherefore, holy brethren, partakers of the heavenly calling, **consider** **[focus all your thoughts on Jesus**—on what He said and did 2,000 years ago, and what He is doing right now for you]** *the Apostle and High Priest of our profession, Christ Jesus;*

Heb 12:1-3

Wherefore seeing we also are compassed about with so great a cloud of witnesses, let us lay aside every weight, and the sin which doth so easily beset us [sally & george thought, talk, action, and emotion]*, and let us run with patience the race that is set before us* [by following what God has put into your heart]*,*

***Looking unto Jesus* [keeping your eyes intently fixed on Jesus, as Peter did when he walked on water and transcended the physical laws, by walking in the new Law of the Spirit of Life—walking by the Power of the Holy Spirit, rather than the old law of sin and death or the law of gravity, which is tied to the law of sin and death]** *the author and finisher of our faith; who for the joy that was set before him endured the cross, despising the shame, and is set down at the right hand of the throne of God.*

For consider him that endured such contradiction of sinners against himself, lest ye be wearied and faint in your minds [by going back into your good and bad, happy and sad, sally or george nature instead of going forth in your Truth-filled and Holy Spirit empowered hearts].

Phil 4:8

> *Finally, brethren, whatsoever things are true, whatsoever things are honest, whatsoever things are just, whatsoever things are pure, whatsoever things are lovely, whatsoever things are of good report; if there be any virtue, and if there be any praise,* **think on these things** **[these are all attributes of Jesus, not a list of things to do, but rather a list of who you are "in Christ"].**

1 Peter 5:8-10

> **Be sober, be vigilant** **[be awake, aware, and alert—stay in your Holy Spirit Truth-filled heart]***; because your adversary the devil, as a roaring lion, walketh about, seeking whom he may devour* [this is not only satan, but also his offspring living within you called sally or george]:

> *Whom resist stedfast* [resist letting your sally or george mind take control of you] *in the faith* [stand firm in your trust in who Jesus is, what He did, and what He said, and who you ARE in Him], *knowing that the same afflictions are accomplished in your brethren that are in the world* [everyone who knows Christ must choose Christ each moment].

> *But the God of all grace, who hath called us unto his eternal glory by Christ Jesus, after that ye have suffered a while* [you have stayed in the weakness and pain without trying to get out of it—this is suffering to sally & george], *make you perfect* [all of Christ in you and controlling you, and none of sally or george controlling you], *stablish, strengthen, settle you* [the purpose of the test is to mature you in Christ Jesus, to grow you stronger in the Power of the Holy Spirit working in your life, because when you are weak in sally or george, you are strong in Him].

1 Thess 5:5-6

> *Ye are all the children* [sons and daughters] *of light, and the children of the day: we are not of the night, nor of darkness.*

> *Therefore let us not sleep, as do others* [being in sally or george]*; but* **let us watch and be sober** [**be alert, awake, and aware, being in Christ and letting the Holy Spirit reveal the Truth and empower you in all situations in your life**].

Eph 6:10-18

> *Finally, my brethren, be strong in the Lord, and in the power of his might.*

> *Put on the whole armour of God, that ye may be able to stand against the wiles* [strategies] *of the devil.*

> *For we wrestle not against flesh and blood* [it is not a physical battle]*, but against principalities, against powers, against the rulers of the darkness of this world, against spiritual wickedness in high places* [a spiritual battle against the devil, demons, and satan's offspring sally & george].

> *Wherefore take unto you the whole armour of God, that ye* **may be able to withstand in the evil day, and having done all, to stand.**

> **Stand therefore** [**stand in who you ARE. In Christ you have become a Family member of God, you are now a We—Christ, the Father, and the Holy Spirit, and you have become One. The "We" is no longer controlled by the I, me, my, mine, sally or george nature**]*, having your loins girt about with truth, and having on the breastplate of righteousness;*

> *And your feet shod with the preparation of the gospel of peace;*

> *Above all, taking the shield of faith* [this is trusting Jesus 100%]*, wherewith ye shall be able to quench all the fiery*

darts of the wicked.

And take the helmet of salvation, and the sword of the Spirit, which is the word of God:

Praying always with all prayer and supplication in the Spirit, and **watching [being alert, awake, and aware in Christ, and listening to the Holy Spirit direct your thoughts and prayers]** *thereunto with all perseverance and supplication for all saints;*

2 Cor 10:3-6

For though we walk in the flesh [we live in a world system run by sallys and georges], *we do not war after the flesh* [we do not fight for our egos like sallys and georges do]:

(For the weapons of our warfare are not carnal [of sally & george], *but mighty through God to the pulling down of strong holds* [of sally & george, and the world controlled by sallys and georges];)

Casting down imaginations [thoughts and arguments of sally or george], *and every high thing that exalteth itself against the knowledge of God* [everything of sally or george, whose ego tries to put herself/himself on the throne of your life instead of keeping Jesus on the throne of your life], *and* **bringing into captivity every thought to the obedience of Christ [waiting for the Holy Spirit to reveal the Truth to set you free from the lie of the mind which keeps you in the bondage of doubt and fear, and in the bondage of time and physicality];**

And having in a readiness to revenge all disobedience [every thought of sally or george], *when your obedience is fulfilled* [to live each moment from your Holy Spirit-filled heart rather than from your fact-filled, knowledge-filled, world-filled, old mind].

In review, here is the plan of God:

- God made us to be one with Him. When the relationship was broken, He set forth a new plan to restore the relationship for eternity. Inside all of us is a desire for God.

- Jesus was the scapegoat; the Lamb of God who would take away the sin of the world and with His body and blood not only pay the price for all past broken covenants, but establish a new unbreakable and everlasting covenant with God. This is why Jesus said, "I AM the Way, the Truth, and the Life, no man cometh unto the Father but by Me." This was not done to establish a religion, but to restore the broken relationship between God and man.

- The Holy Spirit is the final result of this restored relationship— this is God within us every moment of every day, always. This is much better than Adam and Eve, who walked and talked with God, because now God lives inside our hearts. This is the promise and blessing given to Abraham that all nations would be blessed, because all could receive Jesus Christ as their Lord and Savior and all could receive the Holy Spirit of Truth and Power to live in their heart and guide their life journey. This is eternal life in the here and now. This is God's will for our life.

4
WHERE DID SALLY & GEORGE COME FROM?

When did sally & george enter into existence? To understand where sally & george come from, you have to know the story of the beginning of everything as stated in the book of Genesis.

Gen 1:1-3

> *In the beginning God created the heaven and the earth.*
>
> *And the earth was without form, and void; and darkness was upon the face of the deep. And the Spirit of God moved upon the face of the waters.*
>
> *And God said, Let there be light: and there was light.*

This scripture tells us that God created everything by His Word. The creative power in the physical world was and is accomplished by His Holy Spirit. God brings forth the Word, and the Holy Spirit brings the Word into physical existence and reality.

Gen 1:26-31

> *And God said, Let us make man in our image, after our likeness. . .*

So God created man in his own image, in the image of God created he him; male and female created he them.

And God blessed them, . . .

And God said, Behold, I have given you every herb bearing seed, which is upon the face of all the earth, and every tree, in the which is the fruit of a tree yielding seed; to you it shall be for meat [food].

And to every beast of the earth, and to every fowl of the air, and to every thing that creepeth upon the earth, wherein there is life, I have given every green herb for meat [food]*: and it was so.*

And God saw every thing that he had made, and, behold, it was very good. . .

God saw everything He had made, and, behold, it was very good

Man was made male and female and was made in "our image." This refers to the holy trinity of God: God the Father in Heaven who creates and sustains all things, God the Son, who is Jesus Christ who had not yet entered into the physical world, and God the Holy Spirit who is the Power of God in the physical realm.

When the Bible says God blessed them, you must understand what the word "blessed" means. The Hebrew word *barak* means to kneel as an act of adoration to God. In essence, God gives us the ability to adore, appreciate, thank, and praise Him for who He IS. The blessing of the old covenant was that God was with them, and we know this because their needs were always met. As the history of man evolved, the sign of God's people in the old covenant times was prosperity. They always had abundance.

The last thing to note in this part of the story of creation is that when God made man and woman they were created "very good." They were created just the way God wanted them to be; they were perfect.

Gen 2:15-25

> *And the LORD God took the man, and put him into the garden of Eden to dress it and to keep it.*
>
> *And the LORD God commanded the man, saying, Of every tree of the garden thou mayest freely eat:*
>
> *But of the tree of the knowledge of good and evil, thou shalt not eat of it: for in the day that thou eatest thereof thou shalt surely die*
>
> . . .
>
> *And they were both naked, the man and his wife, and were not ashamed.*

Here we see God's first and most important command: do not eat from the tree of the knowledge of good and evil. If you do, you will surely die. As you will see shortly, they did eat from the tree of the knowledge of good and evil, yet they did not die physically until some 900 years later. Their bodies did not die. Did God mean their soul (mind, will, and emotions) would die? Not quite. They still had thoughts, free will, and emotions, so these did not die, although they did change.

If their bodies and souls did not die, what died when they ate from the tree of the knowledge of good and evil? The part of their spirit which communed and communicated with God purely in Truth died. Death can be defined as a separation. Their disobedience led to a separation from the Truth God spoke to their hearts. This led to the birth of the ego-filled nature, sally & george. This ego-filled sally & george no longer worshipped God on the throne of their life, but now worshipped self. Once they disobeyed, they no longer knew the Truth God would speak to their heart because their minds were now in control.

Before they disobeyed they were heart dominant, living from the Truth spoken by God into their heart. After they disobeyed they became mind dominant, living from the five senses, and what they perceived from their minds.

Prior to their act of disobedience by breaking God's first command, they were naked but did not see themselves as naked. They had no need to cover themselves, nor any thought, feeling, emotion, or action. At this point, man and woman were without ego, totally free, and they had God on the throne of their lives.

Gen 3

> *Now the serpent was more subtle than any beast of the field which the LORD God had made. And he said unto the woman,* **Yea, hath God said,** **["did God really say that you cannot eat from any tree?"]** *Ye shall not eat of every tree of the garden?*
>
> *And the woman said unto the serpent, we may eat of the fruit of the trees of the garden:*
>
> *But of the fruit of the tree which is in the midst of the garden, God hath said, Ye shall not eat of it, neither shall ye touch it, lest ye die.*
>
> ***And the serpent said unto the woman, Ye shall not surely die:***
>
> ***For God doth know that in the day ye eat thereof, then your eyes shall be opened, and ye shall be as gods, knowing good and evil.***
>
> ***And when the woman saw that the tree was good for food, and that it was pleasant to the eyes, and a tree to be desired to make one wise, she took of the fruit thereof, and did eat, and gave also unto her husband with her; and he did eat.***
>
> ***And the eyes of them both were opened, and they knew that they were naked; and they sewed fig leaves together, and made themselves aprons.***
>
> *And they heard the voice of the LORD God walking in the garden in the cool of the day:* ***and Adam and his wife hid themselves from the presence of the LORD God amongst the trees of the garden.***

*And the L*ORD *God called unto Adam, and said unto him, Where art thou?*

And he said, I heard thy voice in the garden, and I was afraid, because I was naked; and I hid myself.

And he said, Who told thee that thou wast naked? Hast thou eaten of the tree, whereof I commanded thee that thou shouldest not eat?

And the man said, The woman whom thou gavest to be with me, she gave me of the tree, and I did eat.

*And the L*ORD *God said unto the woman, What is this that thou hast done? And the woman said, The serpent beguiled me, and I did eat.*

. . .

*Unto Adam also and to his wife did the L*ORD *God make coats of skins, and clothed them.*

*And the L*ORD *God said,* **Behold, the man is become as one of us, to know good and evil:** *and now, lest he put forth his hand, and take also of the tree of life, and eat, and live for ever:*

*Therefore the L*ORD *God sent him forth from the garden of Eden, to till the ground from whence he was taken.*

So he drove out the man; and he placed at the east of the garden of Eden Cherubims, and a flaming sword which turned every way, to keep the way of [to guard] *the tree of life.*

This is where the critical change, or turning point, happened in our history. The first covenant relationship with God was at this point broken. Let us see how this occurred and what it means to us today.

Pay particular attention to how the serpent, who represents satan, tempted Eve to disobey God. Once you know how he did this, you will know how he and his followers (demons) and his offspring (the old nature, sally & george) are going to do the same in your life today. The serpent tempted Eve in these four ways:

1. He enticed Eve by first **questioning God's Word. "Did God really say?"** This was his first weapon. It is also the first weapon he will use on you. Had Eve stood strongly on the Truth of what God said, the devil would have had no hold on her, but he is very subtle and sly. he will use all he knows to get you to question the Truth God has spoken into your heart. Had Eve said, "Yes He really said that! Now be gone serpent!" that would have been the end of it, but she did not. Instead, she listened, and in listening to anything other than the Truth God spoke to her, she opened herself to doubt.

Doubt is satan's most powerful weapon. In leading you to doubt God's Word, satan also leads you to doubt what He said is True. The result is a chain reaction. Like dominos falling in a row, once you doubt God's Word, you will doubt His Name, His provision for you, His purpose for your life, and eventually even His relationship with you.

Let us use an analogy to show what even a little doubt can do. If your house has many entryways and a grizzly bear wants to come inside and devour you, how many doors to the house must be open, and how far do they have to be open, for the grizzly to enter the house? The answer, of course, is just one door and a mere sixteenth of an inch would allow the bear to push open the door and destroy you. The bear does not need many doors to be wide open, all that is required is one door opened an extremely small amount, and it is all over for you.

This is what happens when you question the Truth God speaks to your heart. A chain reaction occurs, and one small tiny doubt of what God has said can lead to doubting if He is going to be there for you, and further, all the way to the extreme delusion of questioning God's existence. I'm sure you have heard questions such as "If God loves you so much, why did He allow you to get this disease, allow your relationship to break, your job be taken from you, your children to have these problems?" and so on. So be very alert and guard against doubts about what God has spoken to your heart. satan's greatest desire is for you to deny God and worship self (sally or george) on the throne of your life.

2. The next weapon to be used against Eve, and ultimately you,

is the lie, **"You will not surely die . . ."** Whenever something contrary to what you know in your heart (not the knowledge you have in your mind) is raised, you must immediately take that idea captive and rebuke it with the TRUTH! satan's name is "the father of lies," and lies are his number two weapon after doubt. He will come with lies and doubts such as:

"What if you don't get better?"

"What if treatment does not work? Then what will you do?"

"What if you never find another job? Then what are you going to do?"

"What if this pain never goes away?"

"What if this relationship is not restored?"

"What if this depression never goes away?"

satan wanted to be God and sit on God's throne, so by planting his offspring (sally or george) in you, he also planted disobedience to God and the desire for self to sit on the throne of your life rather than God.

Remember, your Father in Heaven is not a God of "what if"! His Name is Jehovah which, when translated, means "I AM"! He is the great I AM and the answer to all questions. He is the first and the last, the beginning and the end, and everything in between. When your mind puts thoughts of "what if" in your head, you must take them captive and make them obedient to Christ by saying "WHAT IS," and "WHAT IS" is the great I AM.

Here is a list of some of God's Names you can remember when the lie comes:

NAMES OF GOD

JEHOVAH: LORD in the English Bibles (all capitals). **Yahweh** is the covenant name of God. "The Self-Existent One," **"I AM WHO I AM."** I AM YOUR EVERYTHING. **I AM** your provider, **I AM** your healer, **I AM** your strength to go on, to be lifted up, **I AM** the one who sets you apart and makes you holy, **I AM** your peace, **I AM** your righteousness, **I AM** your shepherd, and **I AM** the one who is always there with you. I will never leave you, nor forsake you. **I AM the one who loves you unconditionally and who sees your sin no more.**

JEHOVAH-JIREH	"The Lord will Provide" God always provides each moment. He is the Bread of Life.
JEHOVAH-RAPHA	"The Lord Who Heals" Spiritual, mental, emotional, as well as physical healing. God heals body, soul, and spirit; all levels of man's being.
JEHOVAH-NISSI	"The Lord Our Banner" God on the battlefield doing battle for us.
JEHOVAH-M'KADDESH	"The Lord Who Sanctifies" "To make whole, set apart for holiness." Holy means to be a member of God's Family.
JEHOVAH-SHALOM	"The Lord Our Peace" "Shalom" translated as "peace" means "whole," "finished," "fulfilled," "perfected." Related to "well," as in "welfare." Shalom means the kind of peace resulting from being a whole person in right relationship to God.
JEHOVAH-TSIDKENU	"The Lord Our Righteousness" Our righteousness is in Jesus Christ.
JEHOVAH-ROHI	"The Lord Our Shepherd" He watches over us.
JEHOVAH-SHAMMAH	"The Lord is There" You are never alone.
JEHOVAH-SABAOTH	"The Lord of Hosts" The battle is the Lord's. Jesus already won victory over sin, sickness, and death. You always have the Victory when you are fully "in Christ" in the moment.

3. The third weapon is a by-product of the first two. The product of doubt and belief in the lie is fear.

Doubt + Believing the Lie = Fear

When a person experiences fear, they are operating from sally or george. They are in their old will, old desires, old thoughts and attitudes, old belief systems, and old emotions (fear being just one of them).

In essence, your old nature apart from God, sally or george, was born the moment Adam and Eve disobeyed God and broke the covenant relationship with Him. You know you are in your old nature when you have doubt, and that doubt will lead to fear. Fear always comes when you choose to follow your fact- and five senses-filled mind instead of obeying your Truth-filled heart.

The two trees in the Garden are represented by two laws of God. The Tree of Life is represented by the Law of the Spirit of Life, and the tree of the knowledge of good and evil is represented by the law of sin and death.

4. The fourth weapon satan and sally & george will use against you is truly realized after the third weapon is revealed. It is the ego. Once Adam and Eve had disobeyed God and broken the covenant relationship with Him by eating from the tree of the knowledge of good and evil, we are told:

Gen 3:6-10

> *And when the woman saw that the tree was good for food, and that it was pleasant to the eyes, and a tree to be desired to make one wise, she took of the fruit thereof, and did eat, and gave also unto her husband with her; and he did eat.*
>
> *And the eyes of them both were opened, and they knew that they were naked; and they sewed fig leaves together, and made themselves aprons.*
>
> *And they heard the voice of the LORD God walking in the garden in the cool of the day: and Adam and his wife hid themselves from the presence of the LORD God amongst the*

trees of the garden.

*And the L*ORD *God called unto Adam, and said unto him, Where art thou?*

And he said, I heard thy voice in the garden, and I was afraid, because I was naked; and I hid myself.

Once Adam and Eve disobeyed God, the ego was born. Their eyes were no longer solely on God, but also on themselves. This is why they had to cover themselves and hide from God, and this is why you will cover your disobedience to God (defined as sin) and question if God is really there for you in all circumstances and situations.

What is sin? It is when you operate from your ego-filled mind, when you are in sally or george, believing the lie. The word "sin" means missing the mark. To put it more simply, sin is disobeying the Truth God has revealed to you by choosing your own way rather than His. His Way leads to eternal life in the moment. Your way leads to death—separation from your ability to hear the Truth He speaks to your heart. Once you cannot hear the Truth, it is just a matter of time until that death leads to a progressive dying of the mind and emotions by being filled with doubt and fear. Finally, what you do to the mind you eventually also do to the body.

Truth revealed in the moment is eternal life in the moment. Eternal life can be defined as living in Heaven for eternity, but more important is eternal life in the here and now. This is Heaven coming to earth. This is the Holy Spirit of Truth living in your heart, revealing the Truth in the moment, to set you free from the doubt and fear of the mind. Truth is not a thing or an idea, but a Person—Jesus Christ. The Holy Spirit of Truth will remind us of all that Jesus said so we may walk in His footsteps, being, doing, and saying all He did through the Power of the Holy Spirit. Death is separation from the physical body but is more accurately defined as separation from Truth in the moment.

John 14:26

> *But the Comforter, which is the Holy* [Spirit] *Ghost, whom the Father will send in my name, he shall teach you all things, and bring all things to your remembrance, whatsoever I have said unto you.*

Prov 14:12

> *There is a way which seemeth right unto a man* [to good sally or george], *but the end thereof are the ways of death* [it leads to death of spirit, soul, and body].

How do you choose His Way instead of yours? When Jesus was in the Garden of Gethsemane and was fighting against the devil, He was also fighting His old nature, because He was fully human as well as fully God. He did have an old nature, though He never gave in to it.

Luke 22:42

> *Saying, Father, if thou be willing, remove this cup from me: nevertheless **not my will, but thine, be done.***

Pray this prayer, moment by moment, in your life today:
Not my will, but your will be done Father.
Not my words, but your Word be spoken through me Father.
Not my actions, but your actions be done through me Father.
Not my desires, but your desires be done through me Father.
Not the worldly thoughts in my mind, but let my thoughts be fixed on the Truth you place in my heart Father (as a man thinks in his heart, not his mind, so he is).
Not sally or george on the throne of my life in this moment, but You and You alone Father.

Heb 2:15

> *And deliver them who through* [from the] *fear of death were all their lifetime subject to bondage* [in their sally or george nature apart from Christ].

Ps 23:4

> *Yea, though I walk through the valley of the shadow of death*
> [sally or george thoughts], *I will fear no evil: for thou art*
> *with me* [when I am in You, when I am "in Christ" in this
> moment]; *thy rod and thy staff they comfort me.*

1 Cor 15:56-57

> *The sting of death is sin* [living from sally or george]; *and*
> *the strength of sin is the law* [the tree of the knowledge of
> good and evil—doors 2 and 3].
>
> *But thanks be to God, which giveth us the victory* [over
> sally & george] *through our Lord Jesus Christ.*

James 1:15

> *Then when lust* [the desire of sally or george] *hath con-*
> *ceived, it bringeth forth sin* [thoughts, words, and actions
> of sally or george]: *and sin, when it is finished, bringeth*
> *forth death* [the law of sin and death is evoked].

Rev 3:20-22

> *Behold, I stand at the door, and knock: if any man hear my*
> *voice* [the Truth is knocking on the door of your heart], *and*
> *open the door, I will come in to him, and will sup with him*
> [this is the body of Christ, the Bread of Life, the covenant
> meal], *and he with me.*
>
> ***To him that overcometh* [sally or george in that moment]**
> *will I grant to sit with me in my throne, even as I also over-*
> *came, and am set down with my Father in his throne.*
>
> *He that hath an ear, let him hear what the Spirit saith unto*
> *the churches.*

God your Father in Heaven is standing at the door of your heart,
offering the Truth the Holy Spirit will reveal to set you free from the

bondage of doubt and fear the mind has over you in that moment. A key in this life is to listen for the knock of Truth on the door to your heart, and learn how to open that door in every moment of your life.

What does the Word of God say about opening this door? You must overcome! Overcome what? The power and authority of the mind ruling you through doubt, fear, time, and physicality. What happens when you overcome the mind by opening the door of your heart to the Truth the Holy Spirit speaks to your heart? You gain the right to sit down on the throne of God. You enter Heaven in the moment, you enter the *Shekinah* glory of God in the Holy of Holies, you come to know the Truth which sets you free from all the lies of the mind, you enter the Love, Joy, Peace, and Hope of the Holy Spirit, which is beyond comprehension of the mind. You have brought Heaven to earth in this moment.

Life in the Mud

Let us use a simple analogy. Hard moments in life are like falling in the mud. Your mind does not like the dirty, filthy mud. It hates the mud, and will do anything to get out. Who put you in the mud? Some will say you put yourself there through your own actions. Others say satan did because you were weak and let down your guard. Still others say God put you there indirectly, because He is sovereign and in control of all things. In truth, who put you in the mud is not the question, but, more importantly, what the mud represents: suffering to the old nature, to the mind, to sally & george.

What is the purpose of the mud? To suffer the old nature until its hold over you breaks and God's Truth is revealed in the darkness. Once the Light of revelation shines in the darkness, you will surely "know the Truth and the Truth shall set you free" from the power of the mind.

How do you know the Truth has been revealed and you have been set free from the bondage of the mind? You are OK with the mud, or even better you see the mud as detoxifying or cleansing and you actually enjoy the mud. What the world system and the mind means for evil, God means for good—this is door number 1, not door number 2.

5
WHY ARE SALLY & GEORGE HERE?

Let us revisit the two trees in the Garden of Eden. The Tree of Life represents who you are when you are "in Christ" in your perfect new nature, being the son or daughter of God He created you to be. The tree of the knowledge of good and evil represents your old nature which has broken covenant with God, and has set your ego, your sally or george, upon the throne of your life.

A clue to why sally & george are here comes when we look at the life of the apostle Paul. He clearly states the struggle against the old george nature when he says:

Rom 7:18-20

> *For I know that in me (that is, in my flesh* [george]*,) dwelleth no good thing* [nothing of God lives in george, because george is an offspring of the evil one, and his desire is to set himself on the throne of my life instead of Jesus Christ on the throne]: *for to will is present with me* [my desire to do God's will is within me]; *but how to perform that which is good I find not.*

> *For the good that I would I do not* [because george is preventing the things of God from coming forth]: *but the evil which I would not, that I do* [the things of george, which I despise yet keep doing].

Now if I do that I would not, it is no more I that do it, but sin [I in Christ am not doing these things, but my old george nature, apart from Christ, is doing them in me] *that dwelleth in me.*

But then he finishes his life with these powerful words:

2 Tim 4:6-8

. . .the time of my departure is at hand.

I have fought a good fight [against my george and against the georges and sallys in the world, along with the devil and his demons], *I have finished my course, I have kept the faith* [kept my complete and utter trust in Jesus and Jesus alone as my salvation and my life]:

Henceforth there is laid up for me a crown of righteousness, which the Lord, the righteous judge, shall give me at that day: and not to me only, but unto all them also that love his appearing.

Clearly, Paul had won victory over the old george nature, and since he did, he was able to allow the Holy Spirit to use him to do all God his Father in Heaven created him for; God's will being done on earth as it is in Heaven.

The reason sally & george are here is to remind us we are our Father's first love. His desire is to keep us connected to Him, always knowing we cannot live this life apart from Christ and the indwelling of His Holy Spirit.

Why did our Father in Heaven create the tree of the knowledge of good and evil? Why did He allow the birth of sally & george? He wanted us to know that no matter how hard we try, no matter how much good we do in good sally & george, it would never be enough because it would never be perfect. He said our good works are like filthy rags to Him. The purpose of sally & george was, and still is, to forever let us know that to live this life as God our Father intended is impossible apart from a covenant relationship with the Lord and Savior, Jesus Christ.

The purpose of your old nature is to remind you that no matter how good you are you are not good enough, and no matter how bad you are you are not so bad that the love of God will not set you free from all your sin. When you are in Christ, your communion and communication with God has been restored. You have been made a member of the Family of God and receive all the benefits of a son or daughter of God.

This comes only when you do not trust in anything of yourself or of your old sally or george nature. The command by Jesus is to be perfect as your heavenly Father is perfect, meaning "be fully in Christ." Only through the covenant marriage/relationship with Christ are you made perfect in your Father in Heaven's eyes. When He sees you, He sees the perfection and righteousness of His Son Jesus.

sally & george are here for the same reason the ten commandments and the law were here, to lead us to Christ our Lord and Savior, and to keep us "in Christ" each moment of our life. They are here to keep us weak so that in Him and His Holy Spirit we will be strong. When are people most drawn to God? Is it when things are going their way and they are in control, or when things are falling apart, seem impossible, when no hope exists, and they have no control over the situation? Yes, when things are impossible and we have no hope, we seek God.

If you were God and wanted to keep your children dependent upon your strength and ability instead of their own, you would give them a sally or george to remind them they cannot do it, that their good is not good enough, and that it is OK when they fail in their strength. This is why He is there, to be our Strength in the midst of weakness, to be our Hope in the midst of hopelessness, to be our Joy and Peace in the midst of doubt and fear, to be our Possibility in the midst of impossible circumstances, and to be our Savior when we cannot save ourselves.

So you see, sally & george have a very important place in your life, just as the law did. Their place is to lead you to Christ AND keep you always depending on Christ to save you each moment of your life. This is called eternal life in the moment.

The great Chinese Christian author Watchmen Nee called this eternal life in the moment the "resurrection life." If we are constantly being put to death each moment in our own ability, talent, possibility, and control, then we are also constantly being resurrected and brought into the God the Holy Spirit-directed and empowered life, called eternal life, each moment.

We must crucify, or nail to the cross, the old sally or george nature each moment. Do not trust sally's or george's ability to save you or empower you, or to do anything for you. Additionally, do not be discouraged when sally & george are hopeless and impossible due to how great your sin, blockage, or disobedience. Both the good and the bad must be put to death each moment because in each moment, your mind will try to revive them.

Eternal Life vs. a good life

When you live fully for God, fully from His Holy Spirit and from your Truth-filled heart, you live eternal life. When you live fully for God, but do so from your good and righteous sally or george mind, that is a good life, but with bad attached (when are you good enough?).

Did each of the apostles live a good life, or did they live an eternal life?

They were stoned, beaten, tortured, and crucified. This is not the mind's definition of a good life. But they surely lived the God-desired eternal life.

Eternal life is living as a son or daughter of God, filled with and empowered by the Holy Spirit. It is seeing and hearing everything as Jesus would see and hear. It is saying and doing what Jesus would say and do. It is God's perfect will flowing through you each moment.

A good life is living from the good sally or george mind. It is trying to do your best to please God while also making yourself comfortable, safe, secure, and in control of your life.

You cannot have both eternal life and a good life! To have eternal life is to lay down the good sally or george life. It is to sacrifice your comfortable, safe, secure, and controlled life, so His Power can be made perfect in your life.

• If *you* are in control, His Holy Spirit will not be in Control.

• If *you* are safe and secure, then His Holy Spirit will not be your Security.

• If *you* are comfortable, then His Holy Spirit cannot be your Comfort.

In every moment of your life you must choose either your way (good sally's or george's way) or God's Way. You cannot mix the two. God has some names for when the mind tries to mix the two: double-minded and lukewarm.

Rev 3:15-16

> *I know thy works, that thou art neither cold* [separate from] *nor hot: I would thou wert cold* [not going to do it] *or hot* [doing it 100% from your Truth-filled heart].
>
> *So then because thou art lukewarm* [meaning doing it from your good sally or george religious mind, trying to please God, other people, and yourself at the same time], *and neither cold nor hot, I will spue thee out of my mouth* [God will not tolerate this lukewarm, half in, half out kind of thinking].

James 1:6-8

> *But let him ask in faith* [totally trusting God], *nothing wavering* [not thinking, only knowing the Truth that God has placed in his heart]. *For he that wavereth* [oscillates between his heart and his mind] *is like a wave of the sea driven with the wind and tossed.*
>
> *For let not that man think that he shall receive any thing of the Lord.*
>
> *A double minded man* [a george-driven man rather than a Holy Spirit-empowered man] *is unstable in all his ways.*

On average, you have 70,000 thoughts each day. That is 70,000 times sally or george can try to take control with their good side, or 70,000 times sally or george can discourage and depress you with impossibilities and hopelessness. The solution is found only when we take captive every single one of those 70,000 thoughts and make them obedient to Christ. This is accomplished when we nail good and bad sally or george to the cross in every thought, and keep our eyes fixed on Jesus and Jesus alone. What He said, what He did, where He is now, what He is doing right now, and what He said we will do in His Name. So when sally or george says "I can do it," you must say "that is unacceptable to my Father in Heaven, because it is not His perfection." When sally or george says "this is impossible, I will never be able to do it," you must say "that is true, only in Jesus Christ can We (meaning Christ and me) do all things."

In your life, you have to put every thought or question into one of three categories, one of the three doors. Always ask yourself:

1. Is it God?
2. Is it good?
3. Is it bad?

You actually have only two choices. One is to eat from the Tree of Life, representing your covenant relationship with God your Father in Heaven through your covenant representative Jesus Christ. The other choice is to eat from the tree of the knowledge of good and evil (bad), representing your relationship with your old sally or george nature, apart from a covenant relationship with your Father in Heaven. This is to choose from your mind, leading to good things at times and bad things at other times. Good and bad are connected and have no relationship to God.

The answer is found in following the Truth God places in your heart, no matter the consequences. This is to choose God in the moment.

Following what seems good to your mind (meaning it will benefit you some way, giving you more control, security, or comfort), or not to choose bad (meaning trying to avoid something painful which would take away your control, security, and comfort) are all choices made from your good and bad sally or george mind apart from your new nature "in Christ."

God the Father	good	bad
Jesus—the new and everlasting covenant mediator; the covenant representative.	good, righteous, religious sally & george, your good works.	bad, sinful sally & george, your evil or sinful acts.
The Holy Spirit.	Fallen angels who give power to do apparent good.	Fallen angels who give the power to do evil.
The Tree of Life.	Tree of the knowledge of good.	Tree of the knowledge of evil (bad).
Eternal Life—living fully from the Holy Spirit-directed heart.	Life—living from the good sally or george mind.	Death—living from the bad sally or george mind.
Kingdom of God. Kingdom of Heaven.	Kingdom of the world—good.	Kingdom of the world—evil.
Law of the Spirit of Life.	Law of subtle sin and death—sin of will and thought, not sin of action. Sin of doing good to get something for oneself. All sin leads to death or separation from God.	Law of outright sin and death—sin of will, thought, and action. Sin of doing evil to get something for oneself. All sin leads to death or separation from God.
Jesus is the alpha and the omega, the first and the last, the beginning and the end, the cause and the effect. Christ is all and is in all. He is the Creator and Sustainer of all things.	Positive law of cause and effect—I do good, I get good.	Negative law of cause and effect—I do bad, I get bad.

When we are "in Christ" our sowing is His sowing (death of the old sally or george nature), and our reaping is His reaping—eternal life in each moment in our new nature (the son or daughter of God we were created to be).	Positive law of sowing and reaping—sow good, and you reap good in return.	Negative law of sowing and reaping—sow bad, and you reap bad in return.
Jesus is the Lord over time. He IS Timelessness—the eternal "I AM" God of the moment. God of what IS and what "IS" is a part of His plan.	Things were good last year and will be better next year.	Things were bad last year so they will be worse next year.
It is not about the tumor but about the Lord who rules over all physicality. Jesus is the Lord over the physical realm, mental realm, and spiritual realm. He is the Good News! "Thou couldest have no power at all against me, except it were given thee from above."	The tumor is getting smaller. This is the good news from the tree of the knowledge of good.	The tumor is getting bigger. This is the bad news from the tree of the knowledge of evil (bad).

God has a specific purpose for everything in your life. There are no mistakes or chance in the Tree of Life. When you are living in the moment in your new nature in Christ, you are free from outcome, and free from doing. You are a human being living as One with Him, resting in what Jesus did. You are only a human doing when you are in sally or george, doing everything from the tree of the knowledge of good and evil.

A common lie sally & george use to keep you discouraged and depressed is when you are "in Christ" sally & george should be gone, and if they are not then you must be doing something wrong; you're not holy enough, you have not prayed enough, or you have not read your Bible or gone to church enough.

Here is the truth: once you have entered the covenant with your Father in Heaven and are "in Christ," your old sally or george nature apart from Christ is still constantly trying to dethrone Jesus and regain their place on the throne of your life. They do this by getting you to live "in sally" or "in george" instead of "in Christ." At that time you are living from the tree of the knowledge of good and evil, living from your:

• good and bad
• happy and sad
• I can do it, I have the ability

You are living from your old mind, apart from Christ, instead of living from your heart of Truth in Christ.

People often believe that when they have come to Christ all their old habits, behaviors, and emotions just leave. Many times they do leave temporarily. When you come and enter the covenant marriage relationship with Jesus, you are so in love on your honeymoon that your old nature appears to be gone. But then something happens, the honeymoon ends, and you are back to struggling with your old habits, behaviors, and emotions, just as if Jesus was never in your life. You start to question your covenant relationship and may even go as far to say "Am I even a Christian? Do I even know Jesus Christ?"

You can see how sly the old sally or george nature is. If left unacknowledged it will destroy you. Always remember what the world system, sally & george, and all the sallys and georges in the world meant for evil, God meant for good! So sally & george may appear to make us weak, but this weakness only causes us to run further into our loving Father's arms. His Strength and Power then flows through us. His

Power is made perfect when we are weak in our own sally or george strength, but strong in the Strength of the Holy Spirit within us.

Jesus said, "Thou couldest have no power at all against me, except it were given thee from above." We must never forget our Father in Heaven has a plan and a purpose for everything sally or george is allowed to do, as long as you remember who is in control and do not let sally or george take over.

An example of being "in Christ" but still having the influence of sally or george at the same time is to imagine you have a fear of flying. Getting on a plane, your heart begins to race and your palms start sweating because you are in extreme stress due to fear. This is sally or george in full force. When you enter the marriage covenant with Jesus Christ, you relinquish control of your life over to Christ, and trust in what He did, not in what you can or cannot do. You may think with your good, religious sally or george mind that "if I am now In Christ all the old nature should be gone and the fear of flying should also go away." Yet the fear of flying does not always go away, and as months and years go by, your sally or george speaks louder and louder, saying "what kind of a Christian are you? You cannot even overcome your fear of flying. Are you even 'in Christ,' Is He really there for you?" Or sally or george may use condemnation, saying maybe the sin in your life is why God is not rescuing you from your fear; or because you have not prayed enough or confessed enough this fear is still upon you.

The truth is this: God's power is made perfect in weakness.

Which do you think is more powerful?

To have God take away your fear so you can say "look what the Lord did for me?" Or to have God empower you in the midst of the fear and trembling?

But think of boarding the plane knowing when you are at your weakest, His strength will manifest, and you will always go forth. You do not go forth because the fear is gone, nor because you pushed through with positive thinking or positive profession. You go forward despite your sally or george mind telling you the plane is going to crash and you are going to die, and despite your sally or george producing a state of anxiety and panic within you.

You go forward because **your heart, filled with Truth, knows you must get on that plane.** Although nothing makes sense in your mind, everything is right in your heart, so you get on the plane despite sally or george screaming at you with doubt, panic, and fear. You take the flight, fear and trembling still present, and with sweaty palms and racing heartbeat all the way. This is truly His Power made perfect in your weakness.

We cannot stress enough the importance of understanding our common bond as human beings is being in the Family of God. This bond is having God our Father loving us, having Jesus our Big Brother interceding for us, and having the Holy Spirit comfort and empower us with all Truth. This bond enables us to Persevere and go forth no matter what our sally or george, other sallys and georges, or the world system says.

If you go forth despite the fear (in sally or george) still existing because you are empowered by your Truth-filled heart, how many people does that touch and minister to? Everyone.

We are all weak in our sally or george nature, but we are also all strong in Him and the Power of His Holy Spirit, in spite of our sally or george. The old sally or george mind does not have to change or go away because the heart filled with the Truth and empowered by the Holy Spirit can do all things, even with fear and trembling still present. This is how you will be "in Christ," yet still have sally or george at the same time.

2 Cor 12:7-10

> . . .*there was given to me a thorn in the flesh, the messenger of Satan to buffet me, lest I should be exalted above measure.*
>
> *For this thing I besought the Lord thrice* [three times], *that it might depart from me.*
>
> *And he said unto me,* **My grace is sufficient for thee: for my strength** [Power] **is made perfect in weakness.** *Most gladly therefore will I rather glory in my infirmities* [weak-

nesses], *that the power of Christ may rest upon me.*

Therefore I take pleasure in infirmities [weaknesses], *in reproaches, in necessities, in persecutions, in distresses* [every negative thing that comes against me] *for Christ's sake:* **for when I am weak [in my sally or george nature], then am I strong [in my Christ nature, and empowered by the Holy Spirit].**

Phil 2:12-13

. . .*work out your own salvation* [the battle with sally & george is ongoing] *with fear and trembling.*

For it is God which worketh in you both to will and to do of his good pleasure.

1 Cor 2:3-5

And I was with you in **weakness, and in fear, and in much trembling.**

And my speech and my preaching was not with enticing words of man's wisdom, **but in demonstration of the Spirit and of power** [lives were transformed, the sick were healed, and the dead were raised]*:*

That your faith [trust in God] *should not stand in the wisdom of men, but in the power of God.*

If you have entered the covenant relationship with your Father in Heaven through Jesus Christ your covenant representative, Lord, and Savior, you live with two natures until the day you die. Your true nature is of Jesus Christ, as a son or daughter of God. When you choose this nature in the moment by following your Truth-filled heart, you are fully "in Christ." All He did, and even greater things, you can do by the Power of His Holy Spirit within you.

When you choose to be in your old sally or george mind in the moment, you are choosing to do things yourself, through your own ability or lack thereof, choosing to eat from the tree of the knowledge of good and evil. This blocks the flow of the Holy Spirit, and although you have Christ within you, you are not flowing from your Truth-filled heart.

How can these two natures exist in one body? Jesus spoke of this in a parable:

Matt 13:24-30

. . .The kingdom of heaven is likened unto a man which sowed good seed in his field:

But while men slept, his enemy came and sowed tares among the wheat, and went his way.

But when the blade was sprung up, and brought forth fruit, then appeared the tares also.

So the servants of the householder came and said unto him, Sir, didst not thou sow good seed in thy field? from whence then hath it tares?

He said unto them, An enemy hath done this. The servants said unto him, Wilt thou then that we go and gather them up?

But he said, Nay; lest while ye gather up the tares, ye root up also the wheat with them.

Let both grow together until the harvest: and in the time of harvest I will say to the reapers, Gather ye together first the tares, and bind them in bundles to burn them: but gather the wheat into my barn.

The enemy is the devil, and he sowed the doubt-filled, fear-filled, ego-filled, old sally & george nature in the Garden. When you live constantly separating from the old sally or george nature within you, then at the harvest time when you go to your Father in Heaven, only your new nature will be with you for eternity.

Isa 45:7

> *I form the light, and create darkness: I make peace, and*
> *create evil: I the LORD do all these things.*

Our Father in Heaven created both the Tree of Life and the tree of the knowledge of good and evil. He created your new nature "in Christ" and He allowed the creation of your old sally or george nature apart from Christ.

Ps 139:8

> *If I ascend up into heaven, thou art there: if I make my bed*
> *in hell, behold, thou art there.*

If we choose to live from our Truth-filled heart, being "in Christ," He is there, watching over us. If we choose incorrectly in the moment, and live from sally or george, He is still there, watching over us and using all things to lead us back to Him because He loves us unconditionally.

God's GPS (Global Positioning System)

You must understand God loves you unconditionally and has a plan for you to become the son or daughter of His for which you were created. Just as if you set your car's GPS for a particular destination and accidentally miss your turn, the GPS just reroutes you to your destination. God, your loving Father, continually reroutes the situations in your life until you receive the revelation of Truth He is sending to you, and make the right turn when He says to. His love never gives up and never stops, even when we do.

What does continually, moment by moment, restating your covenant marriage relationship vows, or covenant blood relationship mean?

Continually restating your covenant vows means choosing what God speaks to your heart each moment rather than the comfort, control, security, and pleasure offered by sally or george. You must constant-ly separate from sally or george in each moment of your life, and as Watchman Nee stated, you need to constantly crucify (put to death) sally or george moment by moment in order to live in the fullness of the God life, eternal life in the moment, the resurrection life.

Luke 9:23-24

> *And he said to them all, If any man will come after me, let him deny himself, and take up his cross **daily** [**each mo-ment of the day**], and follow me.*
>
> *For whosoever will save his life shall lose it: but whoso-ever will lose his life for my sake, the same shall save it.*

Watchman Nee received a powerful revelation from the Holy Spirit on how to live eternal life in the moment. The core of his revelation was that only by living a crucified life would one experience the Power of living a resurrected life, a Holy Spirit empowered and directed life.

He realized he had been crucified with Christ; that he no longer lived, but Christ lived in him. He also realized in order to experience the death of Christ he needed to keep the old sally & george nature nailed to the cross.

Although he had been crucified with Christ, **he also had to remain in Christ's crucifixion in his experience, keeping sally & george nailed to the cross each moment.** To remain in Christ's crucifixion is to bear the cross by refusing to allow the old nature of sally or george to leave the cross. In order for him to have such an experience, God must keep things in his life which kept him weak. In His weakness, he would constantly crucify sally & george by going into the fear, the doubt, and the pain, and in so doing would be living in the resurrection Power of the Holy Spirit each moment.

What do you mean when you say sally & george are here to put me to death so I may experience the resurrection life?

Only when you put sally or george to death by going into the pain and suffering, by going into your greatest doubts and fears, will you experience eternal life and the Love, Joy, Peace, Hope, and Truth which comes from the Holy Spirit. The refining fire of God purifies you from the sally or george nature so your new nature "in Christ" reigns supreme in your life.

What is the difference between pain and suffering?

Pain	Suffering
Pain is felt in the We—Christ and me, in your new nature.	Suffering is felt in the old sally or george nature.
Pain is experienced when you go into the weakness of sally or george but do not let them save themselves from the uncomfortable situation.	Suffering is what sally & george experience when being progressively put to death by not letting them save themselves from an uncomfortable situation.
Suffering our old nature causes pain, but only in this suffering of sally & george will we have God's Power made perfect in our weakness (our pain and sally & george suffering).	We only feel suffering when we let sally or george gain control or get a foothold, which can then turn into a stronghold, in our life.
We never suffer when we are "in Christ" in the moment, but instead we feel the pain of our old nature dying to its control over our life.	We always suffer when we are in sally or george, trying to get out of what is by trying to change or control the situation.
In this life, you will have pain as you walk in Jesus' footsteps and follow what God has put into your heart, but this pain or weakness is the precursor to the Power of the Holy Spirit manifesting in your life.	In this life, you will have suffering when you let good and bad, happy and sad sally or george take control, when you follow your mind. There is no Power of God which manifests in sally & george suffering.

Let us use this example: if you are led in your heart to fast from food by drinking only water for a day, you may find this painful and hard to do, but deep in your heart you are led to fast and you know it is a God-directed action which breaks the sally & george strongholds. Fasting is painful to you "in Christ," but you do not suffer because this pain grows you stronger in the Holy Spirit. The pain strips sally's or george's control over your life and gives control back to you "in Christ." On the other hand, fasting causes much suffering to sally & george. They cannot stand the suffering, and will try every moment to discourage you with thoughts such as "this is not good for you, your blood sugar will be thrown out of balance, this is dangerous, something which makes you feel this bad cannot be good for you," etc.

Do you see how the battle works? Going into pain directed by the heart filled with Truth causes suffering to sally & george until their strongholds are broken. In your weakness and pain, God's Power and Truth fully manifest in your life. For when you are weak and in pain and you are suffering sally or george, you are at your strongest in Him and in the utmost Power of the Holy Spirit.

John 12:23-28

> *And Jesus answered them, saying, The hour is come, that the Son of man should be glorified.*
>
> *Verily, verily, I say unto you, Except a corn of wheat fall into the ground and die, it abideth alone: but if it die, it bringeth forth much fruit.*
>
> *He that loveth his life shall lose it; and he that hateth his life in this world shall keep it unto life eternal.*
>
> *If any man serve me, let him follow me; and where I am, there shall also my servant be: if any man serve me, him will my Father honour.*
>
> *Now is my soul troubled; and what shall I say? Father, save me from this hour: but for this cause came I unto this hour* [this is why I came into the world—for this very hour, to do the Father's will].

Father, glorify thy name. Then came there a voice from heaven, saying, I have both glorified it, and will glorify it again.

1 Cor 15:36

. . .that which thou sowest is not quickened [does not come fully alive], *except it die:*

How do you go into the pain and suffer sally & george? By nailing her/him to the cross daily. By laying down everything you have so you may pick up all Jesus gives, which is eternal life in the moment and forever. You cannot mix your abilities, talents, power, and money with Jesus' call in your heart. Your actions must be all His and His Holy Spirit's guidance, and none of yours. The more you have, the harder it can be to break free from your good sally or george ego to follow your heart, because you have to lay down more in order to let Him fully flow through you with eternal life.

This is seen with the rich young ruler who came to Jesus and inquired what he needed to do to receive eternal life. Jesus saw he had come in his good george mind, wanting to receive the greatest treasure of all, but because he came in his mind Jesus offered him the sure Way to receive eternal life. The Way is always of the heart. Jesus told him to sell everything and give it to the poor and to follow Him. This man left sad because he could not overcome his good, righteous, and rich george. He could not follow his heart and go into the pain of nailing his good george to the cross.

Mark 10:17-31

And when he was gone forth into the way, there came one running, and kneeled to him, and asked him, Good Master, what shall I do that I may inherit eternal life?

And Jesus said unto him, Why callest thou me good? there is none good but one, that is, God.

Thou knowest the commandments, Do not commit adultery, Do not kill, Do not steal, Do not bear false witness, Defraud not, Honour thy father and mother.

And he answered and said unto him, Master, all these have I observed from my youth [this man might have kept them outwardly, but as Jesus said, if a person even thinks about sin, it is counted against them as sin].

Then Jesus beholding him loved him [this is so beautiful. Jesus saw how much hold the good george had over this young man, so in His love for the man He presented the action that would have broken him free from the bondage of his good george], *and said unto him, One thing thou lackest: go thy way, sell whatsoever thou hast, and give to the poor, and thou shalt have treasure in heaven: and come, take up the cross* **[nail your good george to the cross and be free from him forever],** *and follow me* **[with your heart, and you will have eternal life].**

And he was sad at that saying, and went away grieved: for he had great possessions.

And Jesus looked round about, and saith unto his disciples, How hardly shall they that have riches enter into the kingdom of God [it is not that they do not have the ability, only that their sallys and georges are very strong, so breaking free is very painful, and very hard to do]*!*

And the disciples were astonished at his words. But Jesus answereth again, and saith unto them, Children, how hard is it for them that trust in riches to enter into the kingdom of God!

It is easier for a camel to go through the eye of a needle, than for a rich man to enter into the kingdom of God.

And they were astonished out of measure, saying among themselves, Who then can be saved?

And Jesus looking upon them saith, With men it is impossi-

ble [because man thinks as a man, not as a man empowered with the Spirit of God], *but not with God: for with God all things are possible.*

Then Peter began to say unto him, Lo, we have left all, and have followed thee.

And Jesus answered and said, Verily I say unto you, There is no man that hath left house, or brethren, or sisters, or father, or mother, or wife, or children, or lands, for my sake, and the gospel's,

But he shall receive an hundredfold [this is eternal life in the here and now] *now in this time, houses, and brethren, and sisters, and mothers, and children, and lands, with persecutions; and in the world to come* [this is eternal life in Heaven] *eternal life.*

But many that are first shall be last; and the last first.

Do only people with many possessions to lay down have pain? Does this mean a person with nothing has an easier life? Yes and no.

A person with nothing has less to let go of, but a person who has no abilities, talents, power, or money has sometimes been living strongly from their "poor me" sally or george ego. These people can be just as self-centered as people who have everything. With nothing, the poor me sally or george can fall into depression and hopelessness, and blame everyone else, including God, for their present state. These people must lay down everything they have, including their depression, hopelessness, and, most of all, their blaming attitude in order to pick up the Love and Grace of Jesus and receive eternal life.

This can be seen in the woman whose difficult life caused her to lead a life of prostitution, but when she heard of Jesus and that whoever laid down their life could receive Him and eternal life, she knew in her heart this was the Way and so she risked everything to come to Him. She likely sold everything she had to buy the expensive ointment she used to anoint Jesus' feet. She laid down everything she had physically, and mentally/emotionally, in order to receive the eternal life Jesus gave.

She did what the rich young ruler was unable to do—she laid it ALL down and followed her heart, no matter the cost, going fully into the pain to suffer sally so much she broke free from her, and received eternal life in the moment and forever.

Luke 7:36-50

> *And one of the Pharisees desired him that he would eat with him. And he went into the Pharisee's house, and sat down to meat.*
>
> *And, behold, a woman in the city, which was a sinner* [a prostitute]*, when she knew that Jesus sat at meat in the Pharisee's house, brought an alabaster box of ointment,*
>
> *And stood at his feet behind him weeping* [because she was repenting from a life ruled by poor sally]*, and began to wash his feet with tears, and did wipe them with the hairs of her head, and kissed his feet, and anointed them with the ointment* [because she knew in her heart that Jesus was her salvation, in Him was eternal life].
>
> *Now when the Pharisee which had bidden him saw it, he spake within himself, saying, This man, if he were a prophet, would have known who and what manner of woman this is that toucheth him: for she is a sinner.*
>
> *And Jesus answering said unto him, Simon, I have somewhat to say unto thee. And he saith, Master, say on.*
>
> *There was a certain creditor which had two debtors: the one owed five hundred pence* [the prostitute was an outright sinner]*, and the other fifty* [others that might be inward sinners of thought, not deed, like the rich young ruler].
>
> *And when they had nothing to pay, he frankly forgave them both. Tell me therefore, which of them will love him most?*
>
> *Simon answered and said, I suppose that he, to whom he forgave most. And he said unto him, Thou hast rightly judged.*

And he turned to the woman, and said unto Simon, Seest thou this woman? I entered into thine house, thou gavest me no water for my feet: but she hath washed my feet with tears, and wiped them with the hairs of her head.

Thou gavest me no kiss: but this woman since the time I came in hath not ceased to kiss my feet.

My head with oil thou didst not anoint: but this woman hath anointed my feet with ointment.

Wherefore I say unto thee, Her sins, which are many, are forgiven; for she loved much [her heart of repentance fully broke free from her poor me sally mind's control, to receive forgiveness and eternal life]: *but to whom little is forgiven, the same loveth little.*

And he said unto her, Thy sins are forgiven.

And they that sat at meat with him began to say within themselves, Who is this that forgiveth sins also?

And he said to the woman, Thy faith [following her heart and trusting in Jesus as her salvation has given her eternal life] *hath saved thee; go in peace* [go with the manifestation of the Holy Spirit, which is Peace].

Know that one thing is expected of you in this life if you are going to follow Jesus in your heart and live an eternal life in the here and now. You must lay down everything in your life each moment. Not a one-time laying down, but a continual laying down. You must continually nail sally or george to the cross each moment. Only in the continual death of sally or george will you experience eternal life each moment in Christ Jesus.

Continually keep sally & george on the cross

By staying in the Love of God the Father and God the Son, you empower God the Holy Spirit to give you His Strength instead of your own, His Truth instead of your facts and knowledge, His Joy instead of your happiness that turns to sadness, His Peace instead of your peacefulness that turns to stress, and His Love instead of your love that turns to doubt and fear.

Who in this life does what they want to do?

Only those who are in their sally or george mind. Even Jesus said "not my will but your will be done Father." So what's the purpose of this life? Is it to be comfortable, stable, secure, and to do what you want to? Or is your purpose to be refined in the fire, as pure gold is, so you can reflect the perfect glory of God—His Love, His Joy, His Peace, His Hope, being seen only when you are at your weakest, and sally & george are the most broken?

This is the Truth which will set people free. Once people receive this revelation, they will go forward into the pain instead of trying to run and resist the pain. The purpose of your life is to come to the end of your good and bad sally or george filled self. The end of sally or george is the beginning of the manifestation in your life of your covenant partner, the Lord Jesus Christ, and the Power of His Holy Spirit. The smile in the face of pain, and laughter in the face of complete hopelessness are God's signature; these are things which make no sense to the mind.

So when hopelessness knocks on the door today because you let sally or george take control, do not fear. Although you let sally or george open the door to this weight in your life, your "Abba" Daddy in Heaven will take your weakness (when you give your weakness fully to Him), and use this very weight to transform a specific part of your character into His image and likeness.

He will make use of every situation where you fail by letting sally or george get the best of you if you give it to your One and only Savior and do not try to save yourself, instead seeking Him until He reveals the Truth which sets you free from the sally or george stronghold. What was weak and broken becomes strong and perfect in Him.

If this is a weight added to the bar in the exercise room, and you know you cannot lift it, all that is required of you is to give your all and never quit—never give up trusting He will do His part no matter how long it takes. He is your covenant partner. He said it was finished 2,000 years ago when the new and everlasting covenant was made. From that point on, the battle is the Lord's. Anything beyond your ability is taken care of by Him once you use up all you have. In all of these sally & george acts in your life, you have become weaker in sally's or george's strength in you. This allows His Holy Spirit of Power and Love to manifest more and more each moment.

Through suffering of sally & george, Perseverance, Character, and Hope are found

Rom 5:1-5

> *Therefore being justified by faith* [trusting God 100%], *we have peace with God through our Lord Jesus Christ:*
>
> *By whom also we have access by faith into this grace wherein we stand, and rejoice in hope of the glory of God.*
>
> *And not only so, but we glory in tribulations* [tests, trials, hardships, and sufferings] *also: knowing that tribulation* [difficult things in our life, or suffering to the sally or george mind] *worketh patience* [Perseverance];
>
> *And patience* [Perseverance], *experience* [the Christ-like nature who we truly are, our true character]; *and experience, hope* [the manifestation of the Holy Spirit's fruit in our life]:
>
> *And hope maketh not ashamed; because the love of God is shed abroad in our hearts by the Holy* [Spirit] *Ghost which is given unto us.*

What do you do when the happiness of the mind dies and the Joy of the Holy Spirit-filled heart has not come yet?

Suffering of the sally or george mind produces Perseverance (this is the Holy Spirit within you enabling you to go on). Perseverance produces experience (this is knowing who you are NOT—sally or george—and waiting on the Holy Spirit to reveal who you ARE IN CHRIST). Experience produces Hope (Love, Joy, Peace)—all the fruit of the Holy Spirit, all the full manifestations of the Holy Spirit of God in your life.

The only way to live in the mud of life is by trusting God. Eventually the mud becomes detoxifying and draws out impurities. When sally & george become loud, you put them to death by staying in the moment rather than trying to save yourself in this moment from what is; by not trying to be in control, in comfort or safety, but instead going into the fire of the mind, knowing only God can save you.

Everything is OK if you have no dreams, hopes, desires, or plans of your own (sally & george). God's will is done one moment at a time, so just stay in the mud until He either takes you out of it or reveals the Truth in it to set you free.

How can you stay in the mud when you experience so much pain? This is when the first manifestation of the Holy Spirit appears in your life. That manifestation is called Perseverance. It is not a product of your positive thinking or strong will. It is a manifestation of the Holy Spirit in your weakness and brokenness.

The anchor of our mind, will, and emotions is Heaven.

Our lot in life is to stay in what is, and let Him reveal all Truth in what is.

Our purpose is eternal life in each moment, fulfilling our destiny as a member of God's Family. This is God's plan.

When sally & george suffer within us, we must remember it is a part of God's plan: suffering leads to the death of the sally or george nature, meaning they have lost all control and authority over us, and that leads to resurrection in the moment, eternal life in the moment, God's full presence and manifestation in the moment.

Suffering exposes sally & george strongholds which need to be demolished.

You cannot have eternal life in the moment without suffering. In order to have eternal life you must put to death the strongholds of the mind that sally & george have in those areas of your life. Dying is the death of the old nature stronghold in your life. Suffering leads to the Holy Spirit's first work in your life—Perseverance.

Perseverance is the ability to stand up to, and remain under, the pressure and continue on. Perseverance leads to experience, proven character, and who you are in Christ, which can only be revealed by the Holy Spirit on His timing. It is also who you are NOT (sally or george), so you are constantly separating from sally or george. As your character and perfection in Christ is revealed, it leads to the Hope that does not disappoint us.

This Hope is the Holy Spirit knowing all things, knowing who you are in Christ, and the revelation of Truth by the Holy Spirit, which sets you free from the doubt, lies, and fear of the old nature. This is having your spiritual eyes and ears fully open to receiving the Truth in this moment, setting you free from the doubt, lies, and fear of sally & george. This is seeing this situation exactly as your Father in Heaven sees it. As Paul says:

1 Cor 13:12

> *For now we see through a glass, darkly; but then face to face: now I know in part; but then shall I know even as also I am known.*

God is not there for me. He does not speak to me or give me a sign!

The Holy Spirit manifests in different ways, but is the same Spirit. The manifestation is not usually all the fruit, or all the possible ways the Holy Spirit could be expressed in the physical, mental, emotional, and spiritual realms at the same time, but rather is the God-chosen fruit of manifestation for that very moment. For example, the Holy Spirit can manifest in any or all of the following:

Love	Joy	Peace	Hope
Truth	Wisdom	Perseverance	Character
Patience	Kindness	Goodness	Faithfulness

Gentleness   Self-control   Power—Creative   Power—Healing
Power—Miracles

He will usually manifest with only one or two of these at a time, and here lies your confusion whether God is with you. He has perhaps not given you a physical sign, has not healed your disease yet, or has not spoken the Word of Truth to your heart. Sometimes in your pain and sally's or george's suffering, He does not manifest in these ways, but instead manifests in the form of Patience and Perseverance.

Maybe that is not how you want God to answer your prayer or manifest in the moment, but you must not forget God's ways are not man's or woman's ways. His thoughts are not your thoughts. His timing is not your timing. He sees the whole picture, and you only see one small part, which is the very reason you must trust Him for who He IS—your loving Father who seeks your best and highest.

Then what am I supposed to do?

Rest in Jesus and what He did at the cross. He is our continual Sabbath rest.

Heb 4:9

> *There remaineth therefore a rest* [Sabbath] *to the people of God* [the sons and daughters of God rest from the work of their good sally or george. They rest instead in the finished Work of Jesus Christ].

This is a rest from attempts to save yourself from what is. It is resting in the pain and allowing sally & george to suffer in the moment. Our good works and our doing something to save ourselves are the same as our love, our holiness, our peace, and our joy. They are garbage because they are done from sally & george in the old tree of the knowledge of good.

Son bathing

But there is something we can do. We do not give ourselves the sun or the tan which comes from bathing in the sun. Just like sun bathing, when we bathe in His presence, His Holy Spirit of Truth fills us and sets us free from the power of the mind, which holds us in bondage through doubt, fear, distraction, time, and physicality. When we are Son bathing, we fill our heart with His Love and Truth, instead of letting our mind be filled with facts and lies which feed our sally or george nature. This is our spiritual Son tan.

Who has the deepest spiritual Son tan?

Who radiates the glory of God the most?

Would those who radiate most be those who do the most work for God, or those who just bask in the Son light of Love and Truth the most?

Who is qualified to get a tan? Everyone. All you have to do is stay in the sun. No work, special qualities, or talents are required. The same is true for a Son tan. This is what our walk with God our Father is by being "in Christ." Gazing upon His glory, basking in His Son light, and sitting at His feet awaiting His Word of Truth to be spoken into our heart by His Holy Spirit.

Spiritual Entrainment

Entrainment is synchronization of two or more rhythmic cycles.

In physics, entrainment theory is the process where two objects, vibrating at different speeds when they are separate, begin to vibrate at the same speed when they are bought close to each other or connected in some way. The object with faster vibration slows down, and the slower object speeds up. The explanation for this phenomenon is that very small amounts of energy are transferred between the two objects if their vibrations or frequencies are not the same. The energy transfer forces the objects to start vibrating at the same speed.

An unhealthy body is often associated with an irregular heartbeat. When this happens, the body can benefit to a large degree by using a pacemaker, which entrains the irregular beat to a regular one.

The heart is the most powerful generator of electromagnetic energy in the human body. The magnetic field produced by the heart is more than 5,000 times greater than the field generated by the mind, and can be detected a number of feet away from the body, in all directions.

With the physics theory of entrainment, one can see how a heart filled with Truth and the energy of the Holy Spirit of God can entrain not only those people around you, but even others around the world.

A lie of the old sally or george mind is that if you spend quiet time seeking God's counsel and you hear nothing, then you were wasting your time, or God was not listening, or even worse, you have sin in your life blocking God from speaking to you. The Truth is found in the concept of entrainment. When you sit at the feet of Jesus, even if the Holy Spirit does not speak the Word of Truth into your heart, even if you do not have any manifestation of the Holy Spirit with Peace, Joy, Hope, etc.—even if you feel in your mind that nothing happened, it is not the truth. To believe that is to believe a lie! When you spend time in His presence, you become as He IS!

If Jesus walked into your bedroom tonight and sat down next to your bed but said nothing, and stared into your eyes with His loving smile, would you say it was a waste of time even though He did not say something to you? Absolutely not! You would say you were in the presence of the Lord of Lords and King of Kings, you were in the very presence of God. What a blessing!

In this life, when we seek God with all our heart, we find Him. When we spend time at His feet, we are entrained to His Love, Joy, Peace, Hope, Truth, Patience, Perseverance, and His likeness. Even if we do not feel them, they are being downloaded into our being. This is the heart-to-heart communion which empowers us to live this life to the full.

Time spent with God is never a waste, no matter what lie your mind tries to tell you. Consider where Jesus is right now, and what He is doing. He is sitting at the right hand of the Father, interceding in prayer that you will become all the Father created you to be, for you to live this moment from your Truth-filled heart being in Him rather than from your fact-, knowledge-, and lie-filled sally or george mind. You can take comfort in this truth. Never did any of Jesus' prayers go unanswered. You cannot fail when you seek Him and stay in His presence.

Only Living in the Moment

How you live in the moment, breaking the mind barrier filled with doubt, fear, distraction, and time, can be seen with a simple illustration of a mortgage loan. Imagine buying a $250,000 house. To purchase this house, you get a 30-year loan. Say the payments are $2,000 per month. Even with all your other expenses, you are fully able to pay this $2,000 per month. The officer at the bank where you secured the loan calls you one day and says you owe $250,000 this month. What would your response be? Would you panic, stress, and be fearful, thinking "I will have to sell everything I have, and ask everyone I know to loan me money so I can pay the $250,000!"?

We believe you would tell the banker a mistake has been made. You may say "I will not pay $250,000 this month. When I secured the loan, the terms of the agreement state I am only responsible for $2,000 per month for 30 years. So if you want to go to court, I will bring my attorney and the documents and prove I'm only responsible for $2,000 per month. That is final."

Just as in this example you are only required to pay one month at a time, and so is it to live only one moment at a time but to live fully in this moment. This is living fully in the eternal life, the I AM present moment. We must quit living in the past "I was" or the future "I will be."

In Christ, we are to live fully in each moment. When you step out of the moment and into the future or past, you enter sally's & george's domain of time. Time past triggers regret, anger, bitterness, and sorrow. Time future triggers doubt, fear, anxiety, stress, and panic.

Some of the things sally or george may say in your mind are:
• What if the pain doesn't go away?
• What if I can't pay my bills this month?
• What if I lose my job?
• What if my spouse divorces me?
• What if I get cancer?

- What if my spouse gets cancer?
- What if my children get an incurable disease?
- What if I never find someone to love?
- What if I never get married?
- If only I had gone to the doctor sooner.
- If only I had saved more money.
- If only I would have married the other person.
- If only I would've budgeted better.
- If only the doctor would have prescribed a stronger medication.
- If only I were smarter.
- If only I had been more beautiful.
- If only I would have planned better.
- If only I would've been more prepared.
- If only I could have seen this coming.
- If only I could have known more.
- I am bored. (Actually, sally or george is bored.)
- I am lonely. (sally or george is lonely.)
- I am fearful. (sally or george is fearful.)
- I am anxious. (sally or george is anxious.)
- I am hopeless. (sally or george is hopeless.)
- I am sad. (sally or george is sad.)
- I need that. (really, sally or george "needs" that.)
- I am jealous. (sally or george is jealous.)
- I am judgmental. (sally or george is judgmental.)
- I am frustrated. (sally or george is frustrated.)
- I blame others. (sally or george blames others.)
- I am doubtful. (sally or george is doubtful.)

To each of these, you must ask yourself, "who am I in Christ?" You have become One with Christ in the new and everlasting covenant of Grace. This means you are no longer "I" but are "We"—Christ and me. You are no longer alone, you have been bought at the most precious price and are now a Family member of God. So let us restate these phrases so Truth is revealed:

- Will Jesus' pain go away? Is He not the healer of all sickness, disease, pain, and suffering?

- Can Jesus pay His bills this month?
- Is Jesus going to lose His job?
- Is Jesus going to divorce His bride?
- Is Jesus going to get cancer?
- Is Jesus' bride going to get cancer when they are IN HIM? Will not Jesus heal His bride?
- Are Jesus' children going to get an incurable disease when they are IN HIM? Will not Jesus heal His children?
- Will Jesus not bring us our perfect spouse because of His love for us?

In the mortgage analogy, the loan officer is your sally or george mind. Those statements and thoughts keep you in the past, in the future, or simply in a lie. The loan officer is threatening you with an old document, the law of sin and death, which is no longer valid in a court of law because a new law, the new covenant "in Christ," the Law of the Spirit of Life, was written and superseded the old law, or the old covenant in good and bad sally & george.

In this court, the Judge is our Father in Heaven, our Counsel or Attorney is the Holy Spirit, and the legal document written in the blood of Jesus Christ is the new and everlasting covenant.

Jesus did everything for us, He died so we may live. In this life, we are progressively dying to the old nature by going into and staying in our weakness so He and His Holy Spirit can live through us.

We must know His unconditional Love, His covenant of Grace, and His new covenant cut in His blood establishes the new Law of the Spirit of Life, superseding all other laws, especially the law of sin and death.

When Jesus said it was finished, He meant the entire old covenant was finished. All works from the old sally & george nature were finished, and now everything is by Grace through faith and trust in Him and what He has done, not in what you can or cannot do through your good or bad sally or george nature.

God gives you a choice:

1. You can live in the Truth that God the Holy Spirit speaks to your heart, eternal life in the moment, which means fighting every mo-

ment, and a life with no pleasure for the sally or george mind. Life will never be happy, good, comfortable, stable, and predictable to the mind, but you will experience the fruit and manifestation of the Holy Spirit, including His Love, Joy, Peace, Hope, Truth, Wisdom, Perseverance, Character, Patience, Kindness, Goodness, Faithfulness, Gentleness, Self-control, Power—Creative, Power—Healing, and Power—Miracles.

2. You can choose the facts, knowledge, and lies sally & george speak to your mind—to live in the tree of the knowledge of good and evil and the law of cause and effect, of sin and death, sowing and reaping. This is striving for happiness, to have a good life, to be comfortable, stable, in control, and to be satisfied. The problem is nothing lasts. The ice cream cone only tastes good for one minute, then it's gone. You're happy today with everything going your way, but tomorrow everything may go against you, and you will be sad. You have a good life now because you have your health, your family, your relationships, enough money, a good job, and financial security. But then you're sad tomorrow when you are diagnosed with cancer, your spouse wants a divorce, your children end up in jail, your investments are lost, or you lose your job and everything in your life is turned upside down. All this is the lie of the mind; this is living from the tree of the knowledge of good and evil.

A better way exists, which is to live from the Tree of Life, to live "in Christ" fully in each moment, to live by the Law of the Spirit of Life, to live totally separate from cause and effect, sowing and reaping, knowing everything is all complete and finished in Christ. Knowing you must fight every moment for what Christ has given you, a life of constant separation with pain, but not suffering. Pain is normal in the separation from sally's or george's strongholds in your life. Suffering is what happens when you step out of your new nature in Christ and back into your old nature. For when you are weak, you are strong in the Family of God. When you are the weakest is when the Power of the Holy Spirit manifests the most in your life.

You must choose: eternal life or life/death, but keep in mind God's ways are not man's ways. Choosing life in your mind is trying to save sally or george in yourself, and that will surely produce death. But choosing the death of sally or george will cause you pain as sally or george are suffered, yet this most assuredly produces eternal life. In putting sally or george to death in the moment, you are walking in the resurrection powered life of Christ within you.

Everything is the opposite of what it appears through the five senses and the sally or george mind. **The only way to experience true unknowable Freedom from the mind, unconditional Love, unspeakable Joy, Peace beyond all understanding, and the Hope which is the anchor of your soul, is to live in the Family of God, knowing your covenant birth rights as a member of the Family of God.** That is when you know Christ is within you who strengthens and enables you to get up and go on one step and one moment at a time. The Holy Spirit is your strength when you are weakened by your old nature. Jesus is who you look to, for He is your covenant representative who walked through hell to get to Heaven.

Once you are living fully "in Christ" each moment, your life becomes a sacrifice of praise and worship. You rest in Him. You are a living sacrifice. You are holy and pleasing to God. You are a living worship to God. You come to realize who you truly are—the We that is Christ and me. The two become One. What do you sacrifice on the altar before God? You are sacrificing and putting to death the good and bad sally or george nature within you.

You cannot know or believe this in your sally or george mind, but only in your heart of Christ. If you believe only in your mind, then when times get tough, you will bow down to the mind. You will try to save yourself.

God wants us to know Him and trust Him in the most intimate way, and that way is through the covenant of Love through His Son, Jesus Christ.

Do not look at negative situations in life as bad things, but as bigger tests, and count them all Joy, just as a weightlifter is excited to put more weight on the bar as he gets stronger. Our greatest test is satan. To pass these tests, you must be worthy and prepared

enough by God, and allow His Holy Spirit to flow through you.

What is God our Father's desire for His children? To rule over all creation as He does. Jesus showed us as He ruled over all creation, including the top fallen angel satan. Jesus said everything He did we would do, and even greater things. Our Father has a plan in everything He does, and if we allow satan to rule the earth because he tricked us with a lie, then our Father will take what was meant for evil and use it to lift His children even higher than they were before. Similarly, His sons and daughters will all be able follow in Jesus' footsteps and rule over all creation, including satan.

The thief comes to steal, kill, and destroy, but Jesus came so you would have eternal life each and every moment. The thief comes to:

1. **Steal**—to take away your blessing which is the Holy Spirit of Truth and Power flowing in your life, by luring you to follow your mind instead of your heart. By following those facts, knowledge, and lies instead of the Truth, you block the Holy Spirit's ability to move in your life because you are strengthening the sally or george mind.

2. **Kill**—the body and/or the mind. To kill your Love, Joy, Peace, and Hope. Doubt leads to belief in the lie, leading to sin which is disobeying the heart and obeying the mind, creating fear, ultimately causing death.

3. **Destroy**—to break your communion with God, your covenant, by urging you to blame God rather than trusting Him.

<u>The power of the devil, of the old mind, the good and bad sally & george mind is the lie, doubt, fear, and distraction. The environments sally & george use are time and physicality.</u>

Distraction is a powerful tool of the enemy. Their goal is to keep you distracted with the things of the world, the things of good sally or george. You must be aware of these distractions and demolish their strongholds by going into your weakness and staying there until the Holy Spirit empowers you with Truth to set you free.

The key to everything in life is "in Christ." He took everything upon Himself and stripped satan and sally & george of their power and authority over you. satan could not destroy Jesus, he could not even keep Him in the grave. When a situation causes you pain, and you suffer your sally or george, you strip them of all the authority of the mind (lie, doubt, fear, distraction, time, physicality, five senses). You make sally or george like a lion with no teeth or claws, only a loud roar. Could the lion kill you? Of course not, unless you let the sally or george mind rule you through fear of the roar. satan, sally, and george have a loud roar, but because of what Jesus did at the cross they have no bite.

1 Peter 5:7-8

> *Casting all your care upon him; for he careth for you* [trusting God totally, because you know how much He loves you].

> *Be sober, be vigilant* [be alert, awake, and aware of the strategies of sally & george, the sallys & georges of the world, the devil, and his demons]; *because your adversary the devil, as a roaring lion, walketh about, seeking whom he may devour:*

Can the devil devour you? Only if you let sally or george take control of the moment instead of letting Christ within you, by the Power of the Holy Spirit, rule in the moment.

6

WHY ARE SALLY & GEORGE SO STRONG, POWERFUL, AND CONTROLLING?

Why do you think our Father in Heaven, who loves us unconditionally, who loves us more than we could ever imagine, who sent His Son to die for us so our covenant relationship with Him could be restored forever, would allow sally & george to be so powerful and controlling over us?

Why would our Father in Heaven allow sally & george the type of power and control that seems impossible to break free from, like a drug or food addiction?

Why didn't God give us an old nature we could have complete victory over? One we could put to death and be done with, or at least one we knew we were overcoming and overpowering?

The reason sally & george have to be so strong and powerful, and seem so controlling and impossible to overcome, is for that very reason—it is "impossible." They seem impossible, and impossible is a concept of the mind, whereas God says all things are possible for those who believe. Believe what? The Truth He speaks to the heart, not the lies sally & george speak to the mind.

So if God's will is for you to become the son or daughter He created you to be, then you will encounter impossibilities placed in every area of your life. Take this into account when you use words such as these:

1. Impossible.
2. I can't possibly do this.
3. This is too strong and powerful for me to overcome.
4. I have absolutely no control over this.
5. This situation is hopeless.
6. I cannot break this hold on me.
7. This addiction has complete control over me.
8. I am too weak to go on.
9. Only a miracle could change this.

These words are from your old sally or george mind. These are beautiful words to God. They represent the end of your self. These words mean you have exhausted every means, avenue, possibility, and thought in your good sally or george mind. These words mean you are at the end of your ability to change what is. This is a beautiful place, and it is in this place the Spirit of God steps in and becomes:

• the Possibility in the impossible.
• the Way when no way exists.
• the Power to overcome when you are powerless.
• the One who is in control of all things when you can control nothing.
• the Hope when you have become hopeless.
• the Savior who breaks the chains of bondage when you are permanently bound.
• the Addiction that breaks all other addictions.
• the Strength to go on when you have become totally weak.
• the Miracle which happens every moment when we are living in Him instead of in sally & george.

For example, if you are diagnosed with cancer and the doctor tells you the treatment only has a 50% success rate, what do you think? You hope you will be one of the 50%—this is hope from your mind.

If, however, the doctor tells you this type of cancer is very aggressive and only 10% survive with treatment, what does your mind say? You are likely to think your outlook is not very good but you could still be one of the 10%.

If the doctor says only 1% survive with this type of cancer, what does your mind say now? You would think survival is still possible; you may have a very slim chance you can still beat this with treatment.

What if the doctor comes in and tells you the cancer you have has never been successfully treated with either standard or alternative medicine? All past studies and all present research have found this to be a 100% incurable disease. Now where does your mind go? Yes, it goes to impossible, to hopelessness. And who do people turn to when things in their life are impossible and hopeless? They turn to God!

When situations are impossible and hopeless to your mind, then the stage is set, so that the mind or your sally or george cannot claim any ability, any part, any doing, or any glory if the impossible becomes Possible, if the hopeless becomes Hope.

Renew your mind to the Truth that He said His Power is made perfect in weakness, and it is not by your good sally or george ability or action, nor by your power, but by His Holy Spirit that His will is done.

Whenever your life seems impossible or hopeless, know they are just signposts of the end of the road for the mind. What does the sign read at the end of the road for the mind?

"Truth-filled hearts only beyond this point."

You know what that feels like, don't you? Going into what seems impossible and hopeless, even though your sally or george mind says you have nothing to gain and everything to lose, yet in your heart you still know you must go forth.

Here is another example: if your child is in the street and a car is coming very quickly and there is no chance that the child can be saved, yet you run out and throw yourself over the child. You know in your mind that you will both die, but you still do it anyway. Who prompted that action, your heart or your mind? Of course it was your heart, because the sign would have said "only hearts allowed beyond this point."

This is the heart of God within you, that does without thinking, that goes forth in the face of the impossible and hopeless, that never quits or gives up, even when the whole world and your sally or george says your situation is impossible or hopeless. The end of your old nature, your old mind, will, desire, and emotions is the beginning of the Holy Spirit working in and through you to empower you in your weakness, in that impossible and hopeless situation.

Does this mean the cancer is healed, the relationship is healed, the depression is completely gone, the fear goes away, and the anxiety completely lifts? Yes and no. As you walk more fully in Him and His Holy Spirit, then His kingdom does come, and His will is done on earth as it is in Heaven. You are empowered by the Spirit of God in the midst of all of these.

The more you are still and know God, the more you sit at His feet listening to His voice, and the more you live from your heart instead of your mind, then the more His kingdom will come, the more His Holy Spirit will manifest in your life, and the more fully the salvation of spirit, soul (mind, will, and emotions), and physical body will manifest in your life.

If you feed something, it grows, and if you starve something, it dies. How do you grow in the Holy Spirit, grow in the Truth to set you free from the fear and doubt of the mind? You must feed upon the Truth and starve the facts and lies. You must fast from the facts and knowledge of the world system.

Remember to put every thought or question in your life into one of the three categories, or doors:

1. Is it God?
2. Is it good?
3. Is it bad?

Never forget that though the choices are God, good, and bad, you truly only have two choices: eat from the Tree of Life, or eat from the tree of the knowledge of good and evil (bad). The choice to eat from the tree of the knowledge of good and evil is to choose from your mind, leading to good things some times, and bad things other times.

Good and bad are connected and have no relationship to God. You find the answer in following the Truth God places in your heart, no matter the consequences, because it is natural and you are compelled to do so. This is to choose God in the moment. Following what seems good to your mind, or to reject the bad, are choices made from your good and bad sally or george mind, apart from your new nature "in Christ."

So how do you grow in Grace and Knowledge?

You grow in these by letting the painful, fearful, and impossible situations in life bring you to the end of your self or the beginning of His Holy Spirit of Truth flowing in your heart.

One of the most important Truths to learn by heart is this:

In life, do not try to get out of painful, stressful, and fearful situations, but seek God's Truth in the situation. When you find the Truth, it will set you free. Free from the facts, lies, fear, doubt, suffering, and stress of the situation. The situation does not have to change—only you have to change, and what changes in you? You are changed by choosing to live moment by moment, seeking Truth in all situations, eating from the Tree of Life to set you free from the lie of the sally or george mind.

Once the Holy Spirit reveals the Truth, you have been set free from the strongholds of the sally or george mind, will, and emotions. This is taking every thought captive and making it obedient to Christ, taking every thought and asking "Is this Truth or lie, is this from my new nature or from my old nature?" It is taking every thought and separating from the facts the lies of the old nature, or when the lies of your old nature are overwhelming, affecting every part of your mind, then you must go right into them. You will now be walking into the fire, because what comes through the fire and out the other side is always a pure heart. The mind will never go through the fire, because it means death.

2 Peter 3:18

> *But grow in grace, and in the knowledge of our Lord and Savior Jesus Christ. . . .*

1 Peter 2:1-3

> *Wherefore laying aside all malice, and all guile, and hypocrisies, and envies, and all evil speakings* [this means to

separate from every thought, action, and word spoken from sally or george],

As newborn babes, desire the sincere milk of the word [this is to grow in who you truly are, a We—Christ and you], *that ye may grow thereby* [letting the Holy Spirit fully control your heart, mind, actions, and words]:

If so be ye have tasted that the Lord is gracious.

Eph 4:14-24

That we henceforth be no more children, tossed to and fro, and carried about with every wind of doctrine, by the sleight of men, and cunning craftiness, whereby they lie in wait to deceive [this is living life from the sally or george mind, will, and emotions];

But speaking the truth in love, may grow up into him in all things, which is the head, even Christ [this is becoming who we ARE, which are men and women filled with and led by the Holy Spirit, being the very image and likeness of Jesus on the planet, members of the Family of God]:

From whom the whole body fitly joined together and compacted by that which every joint supplieth, according to the effectual working in the measure of every part, maketh increase of the body unto the edifying of itself in love.

This I say therefore, and testify in the Lord, that ye henceforth walk not as other Gentiles walk, in the vanity of their mind [this is living from the good ego-filled sally or george mind],

Having the understanding darkened, being alienated from the life of God through the ignorance that is in them, because of the blindness of their heart [when you live from your old mind you are not listening to the Spirit of Truth in your heart, this is called a hardened or cold heart]:

Who being past feeling have given themselves over unto lasciviousness, to work all uncleanness with greediness [once you open the door to sally or george controlling your life, they always seek more—more food, more money, more power, more control, more sex, always more, because they can never be satisfied apart from God].

But ye have not so learned Christ;

If so be that ye have heard him, and have been taught by him, as the truth is in Jesus:

That ye put off concerning the former conversation the old man [separate from sally or george], *which is corrupt according to the deceitful lusts;*

And be renewed in the spirit of your mind;

And that ye put on the new man, which after God is created in righteousness and true holiness [this is the We that is Christ and you!].

Why do I seem to have more sally or george than everyone else?

Two types of people have asked Jesus Christ to be their Lord and Savior:
- The 49 percenters
- The 10 percenters

The 49 percenters are the ones who feel 51% of herself/himself is ruled by Christ and the Holy Spirit, and 49% is ruled by sally or george. These people are always struggling, falling, and wondering why they have such a strong old nature when they love the Lord so much. At times they question their faith and their obedience, and when they are really letting sally or george control them, they even wonder if they know Jesus as their Lord and Savior.

The 10 percenters are the ones who feel sally or george, but do not feel ruled by the old nature. They are aware of their old nature, but it is more natural for them to trust God, to live by faith, and to know God has a plan and purpose in all things. The 10 percenters appear to be closer to God because they seem to struggle much less than the 49 percenters. To this the answer is the spiritual law of opposites. God's ways and thoughts are not man's ways and thoughts, and many times they are the exact opposite.

The truth is this: the 49 percenters, while struggling more and feeling farther apart from God, are actually God's most mighty ministers of His Grace and Truth. How can this be? When I am weak I am strong in Him and His Holy Spirit. A powerful manifestation of the Holy Spirit's Truth and Power is when you Persevere despite weakness.

Think of this: who would minister to you more, the person who stood up and spoke perfectly, with all knowledge on a subject, and using perfect grammar and public speaking techniques, or the person who stood up and spoke with a stutter, who had no worldly knowledge, but spoke the Truth from his heart, in fear and trembling? We are ministered to in the strength of the Holy Spirit which manifests in the weakness of sally or george.

The person who speaks perfectly and is well prepared with facts and knowledge of the world speaks *to our mind.* The person who speaks from the Truth God has revealed to his heart speaks *to our heart.*

The apostle Paul did not necessarily speak with perfect diction, and did not necessarily speak with perfect grammar and fluency, but He did speak with the Power of the Holy Spirit, and miracles occurred.

1 Cor 2:3-5

> *And I was with you in weakness, and in fear, and in much trembling.*
>
> *And my speech and my preaching was not with enticing words of man's wisdom, but in demonstration of the Spirit and of power* [lives were transformed, the sick were healed, and the dead were raised]:
>
> *That your faith should not stand in the wisdom of men, but in the power of God.*

In this life, the only communication that is life changing is heart-to-heart communication.

Heart-to-Heart

The Holy Spirit of Truth speaks only to the heart, because only the heart can understand the Truth of God. The mind will think the Truth is foolish.

1 Cor 1:17-31

> *For Christ sent me not to baptize, but to preach the gospel: not with wisdom of words, lest the cross of Christ should be made of none effect.*
>
> *For the preaching of the cross is to them that perish foolishness; but unto us which are saved it is the power of God.*
>
> *For it is written, I will destroy the wisdom of the wise* [intelligent sally & george], *and will bring to nothing the understanding of the prudent.*
>
> *Where is the wise? where is the scribe? where is the disputer of this world? hath not God made foolish the wisdom of this world* [when you know nothing in your sally or george mind then you can listen to the Holy Spirit speak Truth to your heart]*?*
>
> *For after that in the wisdom of God the world by wisdom knew not God, it pleased God by the foolishness of preaching to save them that believe.*
>
> *For the Jews require a sign* [their religious sally & george minds need a sign from Heaven], *and the Greeks seek after wisdom* [they had very intelligent sallys and georges, so they looked for facts and things that stimulated their minds]*:*
>
> **But we preach Christ crucified, unto the Jews a stumblingblock, and unto the Greeks foolishness;**
>
> **But unto them which are called, both Jews and Greeks,**

Christ the power of God, and the wisdom of God **[we do not preach to the mind with signs or facts, but to the heart with the Power of God that can transform lives from an old nature being ruled by the sally or george mind to a new nature which is ruled by Christ and a Truth-filled, Holy Spirit-filled heart].**

Because the foolishness of God is wiser than men; and the weakness of God is stronger than men.

For ye see your calling, brethren, how that not many wise men after the flesh [you who were called were not mighty in intelligence, wealth, or power, but had hearts that sought after God], *not many mighty, not many noble, are called:*

But God hath chosen the foolish things of the world to confound the wise; and God hath chosen the weak things of the world to confound the things which are mighty;

And base things of the world, and things which are despised, hath God chosen, yea, and things which are not, to bring to nought things that are:

That no flesh should glory in his presence **[no sally or george should boast of who they are, or of what they have done].**

But of him are ye in Christ Jesus, who of God is made unto us wisdom, and righteousness, and sanctification, and redemption:

*That, according as it is written, **He that glorieth, let him glory in the Lord** [the only thing we should boast about is that we have been saved by the Grace of God and we are now in the Family of God because of what Jesus Christ did for us].*

So, heart-to-heart means when the Holy Spirit reveals the Truth into someone's heart, it not only sets them free from the lie of their sally or george, but they can then speak that Truth to another. If the other person receives it in their heart instead of letting their mind block the Truth, then that heart-to-heart communication will set the other person free from the facts and lies of their mind.

The Truth is transferred only through heart-to-heart communication, and the world can be changed only through heart-to-heart communication.

But how do you stand against the strong sallys and georges around you if they are your family?

The answer: you don't. You simply speak the Truth the Holy Spirit has revealed to your heart. You speak it to their hearts, disregarding whatever their sally or george mind may say to you. This is difficult to do, but it can set your family free from the bondage of the sally & george nature.

We must understand that speaking to the heart of someone with a strong sally or george is like going into the fire, because their old nature will try to stimulate your own sally or george instead of letting your Word of Truth penetrate into their heart. If the mind is the gatekeeper to the heart, then the only way to break through is to keep speaking the Truth in Love, regardless of what their sally or george mind is saying back. You must be prepared to Persevere no matter how much their words stimulate your sally or george.

For instance, if a wife has a revelation of who she is in Christ, and the Love of God flows through her by the Power of the Holy Spirit to her husband, but her husband is totally in the world and living from his george nature, then when she speaks the Word of Love to him from her heart, his george mind will try to block this from penetrating into his heart by being strong, harsh, and even rude. His george is trying to block the heart-to-heart communication so he can stimulate her sally reflex, and they will once again be in mind-to-mind instead of heart-to-heart.

As the wife goes forth into the fire or full fury of her husband's george with a pure heart of Christ's Love for him, and as she separates from her sally reflexive nature, and as she Perseveres despite her sally screaming "he cannot talk to you like this, he cannot treat you like this!" she is in the Heart of Truth, which has the Power to break all old nature strongholds.

Finally her husband begins to soften, his heart is fed with Love and Truth, and his mind starts to lose control. The wife has broken through, and Love always prevails when Love never quits, never stops, and never gives up no matter what.

Jesus spoke about this heart-to-heart communication to break the strongholds of the mind.

Matt 5:39-48

> *But I say unto you, That ye resist not evil: but whosoever shall smite thee on thy right cheek, turn to him the other also* [if a sally or george verbally abuses you to stimulate your sally or george, continue speaking and acting from your heart of Love].

> *And if any man will sue thee at the law, and take away thy coat, let him have thy cloak also* [do not give in to the old nature desire within you to speak or act from your sally or george nature].

> *And whosoever shall compel thee to go a mile, go with him twain* [the more you do from your Love- and Truth-filled heart, the more you will break the stronghold their sally or george mind has over their heart].

> *Give to him that asketh thee, and from him that would borrow of thee turn not thou away* [the more you do from your heart of Love and Truth, the more you will begin to feed their heart and break through their sally or george mind].

> *Ye have heard that it hath been said, Thou shalt love thy neighbour, and hate thine enemy* [this is done from good sally or george, the old covenant of law].

> *But I say unto you, Love your enemies, bless them that curse you, do good to them that hate you, and pray for them which despitefully use you, and persecute you* [you

can only do this from your heart of Love and Truth, from your new nature in the Family of God. This is the new covenant of Grace];

That ye may be the children of your Father which is in heaven: for he maketh his sun to rise on the evil and on the good, and sendeth rain on the just and on the unjust.

For if ye love them which love you, what reward have ye? do not even the publicans the same?

And if ye salute your brethren only, what do ye more than others? do not even the publicans so [these are done from good sally or george]?

Be ye therefore perfect, even as your Father which is in heaven is perfect [live 100% from your pure heart of Love and Truth as the son or daughter of God that you are, just as Jesus did when He was on earth. His kingdom come, His will be done on earth as it is in Heaven].

As you can now see, the 49 percenters are the ones who will change the world.

So what is the job of the 10 percenters? Well, their job is not to minister to the rest of the world, who happen to be more 49 percenters than 10 percenters. You cannot minister to the world of 49 percenters if you are a 10 percenter.

Here is an illustration:

If a 10 percenter speaks to another person about eating a health-promoting raw plant food diet, and just says "this is good for your health so just eat it as I do," if the other person is a 49 percenter with a strong sally or george, they will respond in their mind with "what planet is she from?", or "that is much easier said than done," or "she surely does not have food addictions like I do."

If a 49 percenter speaks to that same person about eating the raw plant food diet, but says "eat the food God intended you to eat, and when you need to cheat, chew on the potato chips and then spit them out, or cheat with these transitional foods only after you have eaten the raw plant foods first."

This person speaks the 49 percenter's language. All the 49 percenters who are listening (usually 90% of the people) will say, "she is just like me, she feels what I feel. I think I can eat like this if she coaches me."

That is the key which opens the door to the heart of Truth. God uses heart-to-heart communication, with one person encouraging another from their weakness, and empowers them to go forth in their weakness, being strengthened by His Holy Spirit with Truth and Perseverance.

So, again, what is the job of the 10 percenters? They are here to lift up individual 49 percenters God puts in their life. If the 49 percenters are making the greatest changes in the world, they are the soldiers on the front line in battle. The 10 percenters are the medics on the battlefield, sent to lift the fighting 49 percenters up and help them with their battle wounds. The 10 percenters do not have very strong sally or george natures, but are called by God to speak the Word of Truth in Love and Compassion to lift the 49 percenters back up so they may go fight once again on the sally & george battlefield.

In closing, why are some allowed such a strong sally or george nature? Only with that nature will they walk in the Truth and Power of God's Holy Spirit. Only with that nature will they be empowered to live fully in the moment, because in their weakness God's Power and Truth are revealed. And then those who have been given a strong sally or george are called by God to speak the Truth from their heart to other hearts who also have strong sallys or georges so they, too, may receive the Truth in their hearts, and once received into the heart, the Truth will set them all free from:

1. The bondage of the lie of their sally or george.

2. The other people in the world who are ruled by their sally or george.

3. The world system which operates from the sally & george nature.

Ps 15:1-2

Lord, who shall abide in thy tabernacle [the Holy of Holies]*? who shall dwell in thy holy hill?*

He that walketh uprightly, and worketh righteousness, and speaketh the truth in his heart [this can only be done when you have entered the new and everlasting blood covenant through Jesus Christ and now are a member of the Family of God—God the Father, God the Son, God the Holy Spirit, and YOU!].

John 18:37-38

Pilate therefore said unto him, Art thou a king then? Jesus answered, Thou sayest that I am a king. To this end was I born, and for this cause came I into the world, that I should bear witness unto the truth. Every one that is of the truth heareth my voice.

Pilate saith unto him, What is truth?. . .

The question is not "what is truth?" but instead "who is the Truth?"

John 8:32

And ye shall know the truth [Jesus Christ], *and the truth* [Jesus Christ] *shall make you free.*

The Truth is not an idea, fact, or thing. The Truth is a person, and that person is Jesus Christ. When you enter a covenant relationship with Jesus Christ, the Truth (Jesus Christ) now lives within your heart. The journey in this life is to choose to live from your Truth-filled, Holy Spirit-filled heart, being "in Christ" each moment. When you do this, you will experience eternal life in this moment; His kingdom has come, His will has been done on earth in this moment as it has always been done in Heaven. This is the Father's will for all His sons and daughters. This is the life you were created for and are expected to live right now!

7

IN THE BEGINNING AND IN THE END

In the beginning, God created man from the ground or dirt, and breathed the breath of life and Spirit into the dirt He had formed into man's physical body, and the dirt became alive in body, soul, mind, will, emotion, and spirit. God also created three types of trees in the Garden of Eden. The first tree God created was to be for physical food, the second tree was for man's weakness that would ultimately become God's strength in him, and the third tree was for man's eternal life each moment.

Gen 2:7-9

> And the LORD God formed man of the dust of the ground, and breathed into his nostrils the breath of life; and man became a living soul [body, soul, and spirit].
>
> And the LORD God planted a garden eastward in Eden; and there he put the man whom he had formed.
>
> And out of the ground made the LORD God to grow every tree that is pleasant to the sight, and good for food; the tree of life also in the midst of the garden, and the tree of knowledge of good and evil.

The physical fruit-bearing tree

This tree represents the physical nature of man's existence on earth. Since man was formed from the dust of the earth (dirt) his physical nature required sustenance, which came from the physical fruit-bearing tree in the Garden. God made us with a physical aspect, and as long as we operate from that aspect, we will need physical matter to sustain us. Although we have this physical nature, this is not who we are. We know this through the Word Jesus spoke when He said:

Matt 4:4

> . . .*It is written, Man shall not live by bread alone, but by every word that proceedeth out of the mouth of God.*

The meaning of this verse is clear when you understand the Greek word for alone is *meno,* which means to abide, dwell, be present, remain. This can be translated as "man does not stay in a covenant relationship with or abide in or remain in or continue to dwell in food which represents the physical realm, but on every Word which comes from the mouth of God; the Word of God, the Name of God, and the Spirit of God." Man was created solely to stay in a covenant relationship with, to abide in, to remain in, and to continue to dwell in, God the Father, God the Son—Jesus Christ, and God the Holy Spirit.

Jesus made it clear when He said if we remain and abide in Him, we will have eternal life, which is defined as intimately knowing Him and entering a covenant relationship with God the Father, through the covenant representative Jesus Christ the Son of God, and then being indwelt or filled with the Holy Spirit of God.

John 17:3

> *And this is life eternal, that they might know thee the only true God, and Jesus Christ, whom thou hast sent.*

John 3:15

> *That whosoever believeth in him should not perish, but*

have eternal life.

John 6:54

Whoso eateth my flesh, and drinketh my blood, hath eternal life; and I will raise him up at the last day [this means whoever enters a covenant relationship with God the Father through Jesus Christ will partake in the covenant meal—representing that the two have become One, you are no longer an "I, me, my, mine" sally or george ego-ruled person, but instead have become a true member of the Family of God. You have become a "We"—Christ and you have become One].

John 15:4-5

Abide in me, and I in you. As the branch cannot bear fruit of itself, except it abide in the vine; no more can ye, except ye abide in me.

I am the vine, ye are the branches: He that abideth in me [the person who has entered into a covenant relationship with God the Father through Jesus Christ the covenant representative]*, and I in him, the same bringeth forth much fruit: for without me ye can do nothing* [when you live as a member of the Family of God, you can do all things as Jesus did. But when you have separated from your Family by choosing to live from your sally or george nature apart from Christ, you can do nothing].

John 14:20

. . .I am in my Father, and ye in me, and I in you [this is the Family of God you now are a member of].

John 17:21

> *That they all may be one; as thou, Father, art in me, and*
> *I in thee, that they also may be one in us* [the Family of
> God—the Father, the Son, the Holy Spirit, and the son or
> daughter of God who you ARE]: . . .

The tree of the knowledge of good and evil

The second tree is the tree of the knowledge of good and evil. This tree represents our covenant with satan after we broke the original covenant with God in the Garden. This is a self-directed life, trying to put the "I, me, my, mine" old nature, mind, will, and emotions on the throne of our life. Trying to be God, as satan tries to be God. This tree's ultimate purpose is to show us we cannot live this life apart from God and to lead us back to our Family of God, to be the weakness we need, so we become fully who we are in Him.

This tree also represents our old nature in sally or george apart from Christ, the mental/emotional realm which tries to block all the spiritual blessings of being in the Family of God. This tree within us continues to battle against the Holy Spirit who also lives within us, and at times makes us grow weary in the journey of life. But we must never forget everything God made was good, and everything He created has the ultimate purpose of maturing and transforming us into His perfect son or daughter, and to reflect His glory to the world.

As Joseph found out in his journey, and so we will find out in ours, what the world system, the sallys and georges of the world, and your sally or george mean to steal, kill, and destroy you, are things God your Father, Jesus Christ your Big Brother, and the Holy Spirit within you mean to bless you with the immeasurably more. This test was meant to be the very weight you needed to let all of God's Power and Truth flow through you.

Gen 50:20

> *But as for you, ye thought evil against me; but God meant*
> *it unto good, to bring to pass, as it is this day, to save much*

people alive.

The Tree of Life

The fruit of this Tree is the Bread of Life, which is Jesus, and when we eat of Him, we receive His life, which is eternal life or the God-empowered life that is our choice each and every moment. In eating from the Tree of Life, we enter a covenant relationship with the Family of God, the fruit representing the covenant meal.

John 6:32-35

> *Then Jesus said unto them, Verily, verily, I say unto you, Moses gave you not that bread from heaven; but my Father giveth you the true bread from heaven* [which is Jesus].

> *For the bread of God is he which cometh down from heaven, and giveth life unto the world.*

> *Then said they unto him, Lord, evermore give us this bread.*

> *And Jesus said unto them, I am the bread of life: he that cometh to me shall never hunger; and he that believeth on me shall never thirst* [when you partake in the covenant meal, being fully in Him, then you will be as He is, you will do what He does, and you will say what He says].

John 6:47-51

> *Verily, verily, I say unto you, He that believeth on me hath everlasting life* [eternal life each moment].

> *I am that bread of life.*

> *Your fathers did eat manna in the wilderness, and are dead.*

> *This is the bread which cometh down from heaven, that a man may eat thereof, and not die.*

> *I am the living bread which came down from heaven: if any man eat of this bread, he shall live for ever* [eternal life in

each moment]: *and the bread that I will give is my flesh, which I will give for the life of the world* [to partake in the Family of God's covenant meal means to eat His body and drink His blood, to become One with the Father, the Son, and the Holy Spirit].

1 John 4:17

> . . .*because as he* [Jesus] *is, so are we in this world.*

Our true nature in the Tree of Life, once we enter the covenant relationship with our Family of God, is to do the will of God. To do what God has put into our heart, no matter the cost. This is our food, this is what energizes us, and this is what we live for.

John 4:34

> *Jesus saith unto them, My meat* [food] *is to do the will of him that sent me, and to finish his work.*

John 14:12

> *Verily* [I tell you this is the truth], *verily* [once again, I tell you this is the truth], *I say unto you, He that believeth on me* [if you have entered a covenant relationship with Me, then you are in the Family of God with Me], *the works that I do shall he do also; and greater works than these shall he do; because I go unto my Father.*

Who can do greater miracles than Jesus?
Only those who are in the Family of God.
This is who you are, so stand up and fight the good fight and be the son or daughter your Father in Heaven created you to be in body, mind, and spirit.

Rev 22:13-14

> *I am Alpha and Omega, the beginning and the end, the first and the last.*

> *Blessed are they that do his commandments* [cleanse their garments in the blood of Jesus Christ, entered into the Family of God through Jesus Christ], *that they may have right to* [approach and eat from] *the tree of life, and may enter in through the gates into the* [Holy] *city* [Heaven].

Once you know who you ARE "in Christ" and you know who you are NOT "in sally and in george" then you are ready to fight the good fight of faith. You are ready to fight the battle.

TO BE CONTINUED... **sally & george—The Battle**

8
QUESTIONS AND ANSWERS

Let us look at these important questions:

1. Why did God create a tree that would lead to sin and death?
2. Why did God create a tree that would give you the opportunity to disobey Him and eternally separate from Him?
3. Why did God, who knows all things, put the old tree in the Garden and tell Adam and Eve not to eat from it, when He knew they would and in doing so they would break the covenant relationship with Him?
4. Why not create only the Tree of Life?
5. Why give us a choice that would lead to death and eternal separation from Him?
6. Why did our Father in Heaven create the tree of the knowledge of good and evil that, once eaten from, would give birth to the ego, thoughts, desires, emotions, and will apart from Him?
7. Why did God the Father allow the nature apart from Himself and His nature to exist in the beginning, and to continue to coexist within us?
8. Why are sally & george here?
9. When you decide to follow Christ will all of your old nature be permanently gone?
10. What does continually, moment by moment, restating your covenant marriage relationship vows, or covenant blood relationship

mean?

11. What do you mean when you say sally & george are here to put me to death so I may experience the resurrection life?
12. Who in this life does what they want to do?
13. What do you do when the happiness of the mind dies and the Joy of the Holy Spirit-filled heart has not come yet?
14. Why do I seem to have more sally or george than everyone else?
15. Why must you call your old nature a name other than your own?
16. Why is separation from the old nature so important?
17. What is a Covenant Relationship with God?

The answers can be found in the very nature of God.

1. Why did God create a tree that would lead to sin and death?

Gen 3:22 tells us why:

> And the LORD God said, Behold, the man is become as one of us, to know good and evil. . .

The reason was so His children would be like Him, knowing all things, God, good, and evil. To be like your Father in Heaven, you must see both the Truth and the lie.

2. Why did God create a tree that would give you the opportunity to disobey Him and eternally separate from Him?

God created a tree giving free will so you would not be merely a robot programmed by God. He created you to be a son or daughter of His, and being so you would have the right to choose to follow and obey your Father in Heaven or you could choose not to follow Him and to disobey Him. Without free will we would not be created in God's image and likeness.

3. Why did God, who knows all things, put the old tree in the Garden and tell Adam and Eve not to eat from it, when He knew they would and in doing so they would break the covenant relationship with Him?

God put the old tree in the Garden knowing Adam would break covenant with Him, but also knowing He would restore that covenant one day. He would create a new, better, everlasting covenant between God the Father and God the Son which could never be broken. Jesus paid the price for all the old broken covenants with His blood cutting a new and everlasting covenant with His Father, so when we are "in Christ" we are in all that He IS, and receive all He did. In Him we enter the Family of God. Our Father in Heaven sees our sin (our sally or george thoughts, words, and actions) no more. He sees only His Son Jesus through us when we are "in Christ."

4. Why not create only the Tree of Life?

If God created only a Tree of Life, then He would never be able to show His love for us fully. We would never really have the choice to obey Him from our heart, or to disobey Him from our mind. We would be without free will. Choice means having at least two options. God wanted us to freely choose Him, knowing we weren't forced, but wanted to in our hearts.

5. Why give us a choice that would lead to death and eternal separation from Him?

Once again, without free will, you would never know what is in your heart. You would never know if you would truly choose to obey what He speaks into your heart.

6. Why did our Father in Heaven create the tree of the knowledge of good and evil that, once eaten from, would give birth to the ego, thoughts, desires, emotions, and will apart from Him?

God created the tree which would give birth to the ego, to the "I, me, my, mine," to doubt and fear, to all negative and positive thoughts, to all desires apart from Him, and to all negative and positive emotions because only when we had experienced all the darkness would we truly love and appreciate the Light! How can we truly understand how much God loves us unless we understand the price He was willing to pay for us, and how precious we are to Him? This can be seen in the story told by Jesus about the prodigal son:

Luke 15:11-24

> *And he said, A certain man had two sons:*
>
> *And the younger of them said to his father, Father, give me the portion of goods that falleth to me. And he divided unto them his living.*
>
> *And not many days after the younger son gathered all together, and took his journey into a far country, and there wasted his substance with riotous living.*
>
> *And when he had spent all, there arose a mighty famine in that land; and he began to be in want.*
>
> *And he went and joined himself to a citizen of that country; and he sent him into his fields to feed swine.*
>
> *And he would fain have filled his belly with the husks that the swine did eat: and no man gave unto him.*
>
> *And when he came to himself, he said, How many hired servants of my father's have bread enough and to spare, and I perish with hunger!*
>
> *I will arise and go to my father, and will say unto him, Father, I have sinned against heaven, and before thee,*
>
> *And am no more worthy to be called thy son: make me as one of thy hired servants.*
>
> *And he arose, and came to his father. But when he was yet a great way off, his father saw him, and had compassion, and ran, and fell on his neck, and kissed him.*
>
> **And the son said unto him, Father, I have sinned against heaven, and in thy sight, and am no more worthy to be called thy son [this is our realization we have lived from our sally or george nature and are no longer worthy to be called a son or daughter of God].**
>
> **But the father said to his servants, Bring forth the best**

robe, and put it on him; and put a ring on his hand [the ring symbolizes the family seal, hence the father is saying, "all that I have is still yours." The father does not see the son's old nature, but instead sees only his repentance, asking for forgiveness], *and shoes on his feet:*

And bring hither the fatted calf, and kill it; and let us eat, and be merry:

For this my son was dead, and is alive again; he was lost, and is found. *And they began to be merry.*

7. Why did God the Father allow the nature apart from Himself and His nature to exist in the beginning, and to continue to coexist within us?

God our Father in Heaven has allowed the old nature, sally & george, not only to show how much He loves us but also to show what sacrifice He would make for us:

John 3:16-17

For God so loved the world, that he gave his only begotten Son, that whosoever believeth in him should not perish, but have everlasting life.

For God sent not his Son into the world to condemn the world; but that the world through him might be saved [Jesus came into this world to condemn and judge satan and to set you free from satan's hold over you, to set you free from sally & george].

God wanted to show not only that He loved us as Himself and made us just like Himself, but that He wanted us to experience the true Joy, Thankfulness, and Gratitude of knowing all He had given us by knowing all we are without Him. He allows the sally or george nature to exist within us so we may continually know how great is His Love, His Grace (free gift, not earned or deserved), His sacrifice, and His continually allowing us to have free will to choose Him every moment of our life.

8. Why are sally & george here?

To forever remind us of who we are in Him and who we are apart from Him. To forever help us to keep our eyes on Him, to always give us a choice to be "in Christ," in the new, everlasting and unbreakable covenant with God, or to choose the "I, me, my, mine" ego of sally & george. To always give us the choice of who we want on the throne of our life in each moment. How much more brilliant is the light when we have lived in the dark? How much more precious the Grace revealed when we have lived in the sin of the happy/sad, good/bad sally or george old nature?

9. When you decide to follow Christ will all of your old nature be permanently gone?

No. First, God made us in His own image and likeness, and in being like Him we have free will in deciding each moment of our lives. The most important choice is this: am I going to follow the Truth I know God is speaking into my heart, or am I going to follow the lies, facts, and knowledge sally or george and the world system apart from God are speaking into my sally or george mind?

Second, sally & george play a very important role in your life. They do have a purpose, and they will continue to fulfill their purpose until you are no longer physically present on the planet.

When you choose to be "in Christ" each moment, choosing NOT to be in the flesh or the old nature of sally or george that moment, you are choosing eternal life instead. In doing so, you are constantly crucifying, or putting to death, the sally or george old nature moment by moment.

10. What does continually, moment by moment, restating your covenant marriage relationship vows, or covenant blood relationship mean?

Continually restating your covenant vows means choosing what God speaks to your heart each moment rather than the comfort, control, security, and pleasure offered by sally or george. You must constantly separate from sally or george in each moment of your life, and as Watchman Nee stated, you need to constantly crucify (put to death) sally or george moment by moment in order to live in the fullness of the God life, eternal life in the moment, the resurrection life.

11. What do you mean when you say sally & george are here to put me to death so I may experience the resurrection life?

Only when you put sally or george to death by going into the pain and suffering, by going into your greatest doubts and fears, will you experience eternal life and the Love, Joy, Peace, Hope, and Truth which comes from the Holy Spirit. The refining fire of God purifies you from the sally or george nature so your new nature "in Christ" reigns supreme in your life.

12. Who in this life does what they want to do?

Only those who are in their sally or george mind. Even Jesus said "not my will but your will be done Father." So what's the purpose of this life? Is it to be comfortable, stable, secure, and to do what you want to? Or is your purpose to be refined in the fire, as pure gold is, so you can reflect the perfect glory of God—His Love, His Joy, His Peace, His Hope, being seen only when you are at your weakest, and sally & george are the most broken?

This is the Truth which will set people free. Once people receive this revelation, they will go forward into the pain instead of trying to run and resist the pain. The purpose of your life is to come to the end of your good and bad sally or george filled self. The end of sally or george is the beginning of the manifestation in your life of your covenant partner, the Lord Jesus Christ, and the Power of His Holy Spirit. The smile in the face of pain, and laughter in the face of complete hopelessness are God's signature; these are things which make no sense to the mind.

13. What do you do when the happiness of the mind dies and the Joy of the Holy Spirit-filled heart has not come yet?

Suffering of the sally or george mind produces Perseverance (this is the Holy Spirit within you enabling you to go on). Perseverance produces experience (this is knowing who you are NOT—sally or george—and waiting on the Holy Spirit to reveal who you ARE IN CHRIST). Experience produces Hope (Love, Joy, Peace)—all the fruit of the Holy Spirit, all the full manifestations of the Holy Spirit of God in your life.

The only way to live in the mud of life is by trusting God. Eventually the mud becomes detoxifying and draws out impurities. When sally & george become loud, you put them to death by staying in the moment rather than trying to save yourself in this moment from what is; by not trying to be in control, in comfort or safety, but instead going into the fire of the mind, knowing only God can save you.

Everything is OK if you have no dreams, hopes, desires, or plans of your own (sally & george). God's will is done one moment at a time, so just stay in the mud until He either takes you out of it or reveals the Truth in it to set you free.

How can you stay in the mud when you experience so much pain? This is when the first manifestation of the Holy Spirit appears in your life. That manifestation is called Perseverance. It is not a product of your positive thinking or strong will. It is a manifestation of the Holy Spirit in your weakness and brokenness.

14. Why do I seem to have more sally or george than everyone else?

Two types of people have asked Jesus Christ to be their Lord and Savior:
- The 49 percenters
- The 10 percenters

The 49 percenters are the ones who feel 51% of herself/himself is ruled by Christ and the Holy Spirit, and 49% is ruled by sally or george. These people are always struggling, falling, and wondering why they have such a strong old nature when they love the Lord so much. At times they question their faith and their obedience, and when they are really letting sally or george control them, they even wonder if they know Jesus as their Lord and Savior.

The 10 percenters are the ones who feel sally or george, but do not feel ruled by the old nature. They are aware of their old nature, but it is more natural for them to trust God, to live by faith, and to know God has a plan and purpose in all things. The 10 percenters appear to be closer to God because they seem to struggle much less than the 49 percenters. To this the answer is the spiritual law of opposites. God's ways and thoughts are not man's ways and thoughts, and many times they are the exact opposite.

The truth is this: the 49 percenters, while struggling more and feeling farther apart from God, are actually God's most mighty ministers of His Grace and Truth. How can this be? When I am weak I am strong in Him and His Holy Spirit. A powerful manifestation of the Holy Spirit's Truth and Power is when you Persevere despite weakness.

15. Why must you call your old nature a name other than your own?

You must have a clear-cut separation between who you are in your God nature, being "in Christ," and who you appear to be because of your old nature. This separation must not only be called by a different name, but spoken of by that name. This brings the Truth into the physical realm.

16. Why is separation from the old nature so important?

We are called to be separate from everything which does not honor God our Father in Heaven and glorify Jesus Christ, His Son and our most precious covenant representative to the Father. But let us go deeper with this concept. We are also called to be separate from the old nature within who does not honor our Father in Heaven and glorify Jesus Christ, and who does not put Jesus on the throne of your life (who does not live from their Christ-like new nature as One with the Father in Heaven, but instead lives from their sally or george old nature, the "I, me, my, mine" old nature).

17. What is a Covenant Relationship with God?

God loves you more than you can ever conceive or know in your mind. Everything He does, all He allows into your path in life, has a specific purpose to transform you into His image, for you to become more One with Him. The purpose of everything that happens is for you to know Him better, to become more One with Him in body, mind, and spirit.

9
REVIEW OF 30 KEY CONCEPTS

1. sally & george are random names given to expose our old nature apart from God. They represent living for and from ourselves instead of for and from God.

2. Most people live 95% of their day in their old sally or george nature, and only 5% in their new nature, being "in Christ."

3. The division of who you ARE IN CHRIST, and who you are NOT in sally or george.

Who you are IN CHRIST in your new nature; your mind of Christ, your will of Christ, your desire of Christ, and your emotions of Christ.	Who you are apart from CHRIST in your old nature; old mind, old will, old desires, and old emotions.
Perfect mind of Christ.	Imperfect mind of the old nature.
Do the will of your Father in Heaven.	Do your own will.
Desire of the heart is to do His will.	Desire of the mind is to do your will.

Emotion or energy in motion of compassion and passion for what He puts into your heart.	Emotion or energy in motion of pleasure, gratification, and happiness that drives your mind.

4. In the Garden of Eden were two trees, the Tree of Life and the tree of the knowledge of good and evil. These two trees represent the whole human journey and experience.

• **The Tree of Life**—represents your covenant relationship with God your Father in Heaven, and also living a heart-directed life in and from Him. This is the We—the Christ and me who have become One—like a covenant marriage relationship where the two have become one, or a blood brother relationship where the two have become one.

• **The tree of the knowledge of good and evil (bad)**—represents our covenant with satan after breaking our original covenant with God in the Garden. This is a self-directed life trying to put the "I, me, my, mine" old nature, mind, will, desires, and emotions on the throne of your life. It is trying to be God as satan tries to be God.

The tree of the knowledge of good and evil's ultimate purpose is to show us we cannot live this life apart from God. This leads us back to God the Father through the Savior, who is Jesus Christ.

5. In life, you have three choices, but actually just two. You can choose God, good, or bad. However, we have noted that good and bad are actually one choice together. You may choose the Tree of Life in this moment, or you may choose the tree of the knowledge of good and evil (bad). Simply stated, you have three doors to choose from: door number 1 is God, door number 2 is the good side of the tree of knowledge of good and evil (bad), and door number 3 is the bad, or evil, side of the tree of knowledge of good and evil. So think which door—number 1, 2, or 3—you are going to choose with everything that comes into your life?

Here is an example: A person fasts and prays, expecting God to hear his prayer. Which door he in? It is door number 2 because he is doing something good to get something in return. This is living in cause and effect, sowing and reaping.

Another example: A person has very low self-esteem, feeling like they will never accomplish anything in life because they lack any talent or ability. Which door is it? Door number 3.

How about this example: A person feels an overwhelming Peace in making a decision that should not be peaceful. Their thoughts tell of all they will lose if they go forward with this decision, yet they still have a Peace they cannot explain. Which door is this? That is right, door number 1. So remember to always be aware of what door you are in or what tree you are in.

Door Number 1	Door Number 2	Door Number 3
Tree of Life	Tree of knowledge of good	Tree of knowledge of evil (bad)
God	good	bad
Eternal Life	life	death
Joy unspeakable	happy	sad
Peace that transcends all understanding	peaceful	stressful
Unconditional Love	conditional love	hate
Hope in Him, the anchor of our soul, the rock	hopeful	hopeless
Truth	fact	lie
Know that you know that you know	knowledge	doubt
Trust	courage	fear
Covenant relationship with God through Christ	religion	evil

6. In your life, you have to put every thought or question into one of three categories, one of the three doors. Always ask yourself:
- Is it God?
- Is it good?
- Is it bad?

You actually have only two choices. One is to eat from the Tree of Life, representing your covenant relationship with God your Father in Heaven through your covenant representative Jesus Christ. The other choice is to eat from the tree of the knowledge of good and evil (bad), representing your relationship with your old sally or george nature, apart from a covenant relationship with your Father in Heaven. This is to choose from your mind, leading to good things at times and bad things at other times. Good and bad are connected and have no relationship to God.

The answer is found in following the Truth God places in your heart, no matter the consequences. This is to choose God in the moment.

Following what seems good to your mind (meaning it will benefit you some way, giving you more control, security, or comfort), or not to choose bad (meaning trying to avoid something painful which would take away your control, security, and comfort) are all choices made from your good and bad sally or george mind apart from your new nature "in Christ."

God the Father	good	bad
Jesus—the new and everlasting covenant mediator; the covenant representative.	good, righteous, religious sally & george, your good works.	bad, sinful sally & george, your evil or sinful acts.
The Holy Spirit.	Fallen angels who give power to do apparent good.	Fallen angels who give the power to do evil.
The Tree of Life.	Tree of the knowledge of good.	Tree of the knowledge of evil (bad).
Eternal Life—living fully from the Holy Spirit-directed heart.	Life—living from the good sally or george mind.	Death—living from the bad sally or george mind.
Kingdom of God. Kingdom of Heaven.	Kingdom of the world—good.	Kingdom of the world—evil.

Law of the Spirit of Life.	Law of subtle sin and death—sin of will and thought, not sin of action. Sin of doing good to get something for oneself. All sin leads to death or separation from God.	Law of outright sin and death—sin of will, thought, and action. Sin of doing evil to get something for oneself. All sin leads to death or separation from God.
Jesus is the alpha and the omega, the first and the last, the beginning and the end, the cause and the effect. Christ is all and is in all. He is the Creator and Sustainer of all things.	Positive law of cause and effect—I do good, I get good.	Negative law of cause and effect—I do bad, I get bad.
When we are "in Christ" our sowing is His sowing (death of the old sally or george nature), and our reaping is His reaping—eternal life in each moment in our new nature (the son or daughter of God we were created to be).	Positive law of sowing and reaping—sow good, and you reap good in return.	Negative law of sowing and reaping—sow bad, and you reap bad in return.
Jesus is the Lord over time. He IS Timelessness—the eternal "I AM" God of the moment. God of what IS and what "IS" is a part of His plan.	Things were good last year and will be better next year.	Things were bad last year so they will be worse next year.

It is not about the tumor but about the Lord who rules over all physicality. Jesus is the Lord over the physical realm, mental realm, and spiritual realm. He is the Good News! "Thou couldest have no power at all against me, except it were given thee from above."	The tumor is getting smaller. This is the good news from the tree of the knowledge of good.	The tumor is getting bigger. This is the bad news from the tree of the knowledge of evil (bad).

7. Our purpose is to stay in what is and let Him reveal all Truth in what is.

When sally & george suffer within us, we must remember it is a part of God's plan: suffering leads to the death of the sally or george nature, meaning they have lost all control and authority over us, and that leads to resurrection in the moment, eternal life in the moment, God's full presence and manifestation in the moment.

8. Suffering exposes sally & george strongholds which need to be demolished.

You cannot have eternal life in the moment without suffering. In order to have eternal life you must put to death the strongholds of the mind that sally & george have in those areas of your life. Dying is the death of the old nature stronghold in your life. Suffering leads to the Holy Spirit's first work in your life—Perseverance.

9. What is the difference between pain and suffering?

Pain	Suffering
Pain is felt in the We—Christ and me, in your new nature.	Suffering is felt in the old sally or george nature.

Pain is experienced when you go into the weakness of sally or george but do not let them save themselves from the uncomfortable situation.	Suffering is what sally & george experience when being progressively put to death by not letting them save themselves from an uncomfortable situation.
Suffering our old nature causes pain, but only in this suffering of sally & george will we have God's Power made perfect in our weakness (our pain and sally & george suffering).	We only feel suffering when we let sally or george gain control or get a foothold, which can then turn into a stronghold, in our life.
We never suffer when we are "in Christ" in the moment, but instead we feel the pain of our old nature dying to its control over our life.	We always suffer when we are in sally or george, trying to get out of what is by trying to change or control the situation.
In this life, you will have pain as you walk in Jesus' footsteps and follow what God has put into your heart, but this pain or weakness is the precursor to the Power of the Holy Spirit manifesting in your life.	In this life, you will have suffering when you let good and bad, happy and sad sally or george take control, when you follow your mind. There is no Power of God which manifests in sally & george suffering.

10. The battle is going into the pain directed by the heart filled with Truth, causing suffering to sally & george until their strongholds are broken.

11. sally & george are here to put you to death so you may experience the resurrection life.

Only when you put sally or george to death by going into the pain and suffering, by going into your greatest doubts and fears, will you experience eternal life and the Love, Joy, Peace, Hope, and Truth which comes from the Holy Spirit. The refining fire of God purifies you from the sally or george nature so your new nature "in Christ" reigns supreme in your life. The resurrected life can only come with a crucified life. We cannot experience the power of resurrection unless we continually crucify our old nature.

12. Knowing these truths enables you to live a life of Victory and Freedom in Christ:
- In your weakness is where His strength, His Holy Spirit, manifests.
- No condemnation exists for those who are in Christ Jesus.
- Nothing can ever separate you from the Love of God.

13. sally & george are here for the same reason the ten commandments and the law were here, to lead us to Christ our Lord and Savior, and to keep us "in Christ" each moment of our life. They are here to keep us weak so that in Him and His Holy Spirit we will be strong. sally & george are here to keep us always depending on Christ to save us each moment of our life.

14. The power of the devil, of the old mind, the good and bad sally & george mind is the lie, doubt, fear, and distraction. The environments sally & george use are time and physicality.

15. Distraction is a powerful tool of the enemy. Their goal is to keep you distracted with the things of the world, the things of good sally or george. You must be aware of these distractions and demolish their strongholds by going into your weakness and staying there until the Holy Spirit empowers you with Truth to set you free.

16. You will be tempted by sally or george in these four ways:
- **The first weapon is questioning God's Word spoken to your heart. Doubt is sally or georges most powerful weapon.** In leading you to doubt God's Word, sally or george will also lead you to doubt what He said is True. The result is a chain reaction. Like dominos falling in a row, once you doubt God's Word, you will doubt His Name, His provision for you, His purpose for your life, and eventually even His relationship with you.
- **The next weapon to be used is the lie.**

Whenever something contrary to what you know in your heart (not the knowledge you have in your mind) is raised, you must immediately take that idea captive and rebuke it with the TRUTH! satan's name is "the father of lies," and lies are sally's or george's number two weapon after doubt. sally or george want to sit on the throne of your life. Remember, your Father in Heaven is not a God of "what if"! His Name is Jehovah which, when translated, means "I AM"! He is the great I AM and the answer to all questions. He is the first and the last, the beginning and the end, and everything in between. When your mind puts thoughts of "what if" in your head, you must take them captive and make them obedient to Christ by saying "WHAT IS," and "WHAT IS" is the great I AM.

- **The third weapon is a by-product of the first two. The product of doubt and belief in the lie is fear.**
  Doubt + Believing the Lie = Fear
  When a person experiences fear, they are operating from sally or george. They are in their old will, old desires, old thoughts and attitudes, old belief systems, and old emotions (fear being just one of them).
  You know you are in your old nature when you have doubt, and that doubt will lead to fear. Fear always comes when you choose to follow your fact- and five senses-filled mind instead of obeying your Truth-filled heart.

- **The fourth weapon satan and sally & george will use against you is truly realized after the third weapon is revealed. It is the ego.** The sally & george ego desires to control your life completely. They will always oppose the Truth God speaks to your heart. The ego is self-centered not God centered.

17. Truth revealed in the moment is eternal life in the moment. Eternal life can be defined as living in Heaven for eternity, but more important is eternal life in the here and now. This is Heaven coming to earth.

This is the Holy Spirit of Truth living in your heart, revealing the Truth in the moment, to set you free from the doubt and fear of the mind.

18. The Holy Spirit of Truth will remind us of all that Jesus said so we may walk in His footsteps, being, doing, and saying all He did through the Power of the Holy Spirit. Death is separation from the physical body, but is more accurately defined as separation from Truth in the moment.

19. God's GPS (Global Positioning System)

You must understand God loves you unconditionally and has a plan for you to become the son or daughter of His for which you were created. Just as if you set your car's GPS for a particular destination and accidentally miss your turn, the GPS just reroutes you to your destination. God, your loving Father, continually reroutes the situations in your life until you receive the revelation of Truth He is sending to you, and make the right turn when He says to. His love never gives up and never stops, even when we do.

20. Son bathing

We do not give ourselves the sun or the tan which comes from bathing in the sun. Just like sun bathing, when we bathe in His presence, His Holy Spirit of Truth fills us and sets us free from the power of the mind, which holds us in bondage through doubt, fear, distraction, time, and physicality. When we are Son bathing, we fill our heart with His Love and Truth, instead of letting our mind be filled with facts and lies which feed our sally or george nature. This is our spiritual Son tan.

21. Not Just Once

This decision to be "in Christ" has to be made every moment of your life after you receive Him as your Lord and Savior (Lord meaning He is your covenant representative to the Father in Heaven, He is your everything; and Savior meaning only His cutting the new and everlasting covenant allows you to be set free from your sally or george nature).

To be "clothed with Christ" is not a one-time decision. Instead, you are to put Him on or wear Him each moment of your life by following the Truth your Father in Heaven speaks to your heart through the Holy Spirit. Each moment you can choose eternal life "in Christ," or you can choose death by following the old sally or george mind.

22. Jesus did everything for us. He died so we may live. In this life, we are progressively dying to the old nature by going into and staying in our weakness so He and His Holy Spirit can live through us.

23. The only way to experience true unknowable Freedom from the mind, unconditional Love, unspeakable Joy, Peace beyond all understanding, and the Hope which is the anchor of your soul, is to live in the Family of God, knowing your covenant birth rights as a member of the Family of God.

24. We cannot stress enough the importance of understanding our common bond as human beings is being in the Family of God. This bond is having God our Father loving us, having Jesus our Big Brother interceding for us, and having the Holy Spirit comfort and empower us with all Truth. This bond enables us to Persevere and go forth no matter what our sally or george, other sallys and georges, or the world system says.

25. Do not look at negative situations in life as bad things, but as bigger tests, and count them all Joy, just as a weightlifter is excited to put more weight on the bar as he gets stronger. Our greatest test is satan. To pass these tests, you must be worthy and prepared enough by God, and allow His Holy Spirit to flow through you.

26. Life in the Mud

Hard moments in life are like falling in the mud. Your mind does not like the dirty, filthy mud. It hates the mud, and will do anything to get out. Who put you in the mud? Some will say you put yourself there through your own actions. Others say satan did, because you were weak and let down your guard. Still others say God put you there indirectly, because He is sovereign and in control of all things. In truth, who put you in the mud is not the question, but more importantly what the mud represents: suffering to the old nature, to the mind, to sally & george.

What is the purpose of the mud? To suffer the old nature until its hold over you breaks and God's Truth is revealed in the darkness. Once the Light of revelation shines in the darkness, you will surely "know the Truth and the Truth shall set you free" from the power of the mind.

How do you know the Truth has been revealed and you have been set free from the bondage of the mind? You are OK with the mud, or even better you see the mud as detoxifying or cleansing and you actually enjoy the mud. What the world system and the mind means for evil, God means for good—this is door number 1, not door number 2.

27. One of the most important Truths to learn by heart is this:

In life, do not try to get out of painful, stressful, and fearful situations, but seek God's Truth in the situation. When you find the Truth, it will set you free. Free from the facts, lies, fear, doubt, suffering, and stress of the situation. The situation does not have to change—only you have to change, and what changes in you? You are changed by choosing to live moment by moment, seeking Truth in all situations, eating from the Tree of Life to set you free from the lie of the sally or george mind.

Once the Holy Spirit reveals the Truth, you have been set free from the strongholds of the sally or george mind, will, and emotions. This is taking every thought captive and making it obedient to Christ, taking every thought and asking "Is this Truth or lie, is this from my new nature or from my old nature?" It is taking every thought and separating from the facts the lies of the old nature, or when the lies of your old nature are overwhelming, affecting every part of your mind, then you must go right into them. You will now be walking into the fire, because what comes through the fire and out the other side is always a pure heart. The mind will never go through the fire, because it means death.

28. Heart-to-Heart

In this life, the only communication that is life changing is heart-to-heart communication.

The Holy Spirit of Truth speaks only to the heart, because only the heart can understand the Truth of God. The mind will think the Truth is foolish.

So, heart-to-heart means when the Holy Spirit reveals the Truth into someone's heart, it not only sets them free from the lie of their sally or george, but they can then speak that Truth to another. If the other person receives it in their heart instead of letting their mind block the Truth, then that heart-to-heart communication will set the other person free from the facts and lies of their mind.

The Truth is transferred only through heart-to-heart communication, and the world can be changed only through heart-to-heart communication.

29. The Truth is not an idea, fact, or thing. The Truth is a person, and that person is Jesus Christ.

When you enter a covenant relationship with Jesus Christ, the Truth (Jesus Christ) now lives within your heart. The journey in this life is to choose to live from your Truth-filled, Holy Spirit-filled heart, being "in Christ" each moment. When you do this, you will experience eternal life in this moment; His kingdom has come, His will has been done on earth in this moment, as it has always been done in Heaven. This is the Father's will for all His sons and daughters. This is the life you were created for and are expected to live right now!

30. In Summary

You have two natures if you have entered the new and everlasting covenant with God your Father in Heaven through the atoning sacrifice of Jesus Christ, your Lord and Savior. Your new nature in Christ is your perfect God nature which makes you a son or daughter of God. Your new nature adopts you into the Family of God, making you an heir along with Christ. This nature is led and empowered by the Holy Spirit of God. Your new nature must be actively chosen through your free will each moment, so the blessing of Abraham, which is the Holy Spirit, can flow through your thoughts, actions, and words each and every moment.

In review, here is the plan of God:

God made us to be one with Him. When the relationship was broken, He set forth a new plan to restore the relationship for eternity. Inside all of us is a desire for God.

Jesus was the scapegoat; the Lamb of God who would take away the sin of the world and with His body and blood not only pay the price for all past broken covenants, but establish a new unbreakable and ever-lasting covenant with God. This is why Jesus said "I AM the Way, the Truth, and the Life, no man cometh unto the Father but by Me." This was not done to establish a religion, but to restore the broken relationship between God and man.

The Holy Spirit is the final result of this restored relationship—this is God within us every moment of every day, always. This is much better than Adam and Eve, who walked and talked with God, because now God lives inside our hearts. This is the promise and blessing given to Abraham that all nations would be blessed, because all could receive Jesus Christ as their Lord and Savior, and all could receive the Holy Spirit of Truth and Power to live in their heart and guide their life journey. This is eternal life in the here and now. This is God's will for our life.